Oil Painting Medic

How Can I Inspire my Painting Class?
Black & White Edition

Lesson Plan Ideas for Oil Painting in Post Compulsory Education & an Essential Guide to Teaching

Rachel Shirley

First Published in 2011 by Rachel Shirley
Text, photographs and illustrations © Rachel Shirley 2011

ISBN-13:978-1469929118
ISBN-10:1469929112

All rights reserved

The Right of Rachel Shirley to be identified as the author of this work has been asserted in accordance with the Copyright Designs and Patents Act 1988 Section 77 and 78.

No part of this publication may be republished, stored in a retrieval system or transmitted in any form or by any means without the prior permission of the copyright owner.

This book is sold subject to the conditions that all designs are copyright and are not for the commercial reproduction without the written permission of the designer and copyright owner.

While every effort has been made to represent the colours accurately, guarantee cannot be given that they are an exact match to the pigments.

To my sister Ruth

How Can I Inspire my Painting Class?
Black & White Edition

Lesson Plan Ideas for Oil Painting in Post Compulsory Education & an Essential Guide to Teaching

Rachel Shirley

Contents

Introduction — 8

i Guide to art materials

1. Art materials needed for oil painting — 10

ii Students' needs

2. Multi-sensory art lesson planning — 20
3. The individual learning plan and differentiation — 22
4. Motivating art students — 24
5. Encouraging the reluctant art student — 26
6. Students with special needs — 28

iii Preparing to teach art

7. The initial assessment for lesson planning — 30
8. The scheme of work for oil painting — 33
9. Selecting the theme for the course — 35
10. Writing objectives for art lessons — 38
11. Independent learning in art class: Behaviourism versus Cognitivism — 42
12. Icebreaker ideas — 45

iv The initial lessons

13. The first painting class — 48
14. The definition of painting — 51

v Lessons to underpin painting

15	Distorted perception in drawing	54
16	Ways to improve drawing	57
17	Taking a line for a walk part 1: Random mark-making	61
18	Taking a line for a walk part 2: Emulating Expressionism	63
19	The artist's viewfinder	65
20	Negative space and positive shapes	68
21	Increments of tones	70
22	Using photographs for painting	72

vi Lessons on colour use

23	Introduction to colour theory	76
24	Darkening colours with complimentaries	80
25	Mixing greys and neutral colours	82

vii Lessons exploring painting techniques

26	Painting dark to light	84
27	Alla prima painting	87
28	Painting wet into wet	90
29	Impasto oil painting	92
30	Emulating the Impressionists	94
31	Using palette knives	97
32	Sgraffito oil painting	99

viii Lessons on still life painting

33	Composing a still life	101
34	Reflected light on a spheroid	104
35	Shadows in still life	106
36	Painting ellipses	108
37	Objects in foreshortening	111
38	Painting reflections	113
39	Painting flowers	116
40	Painting aged objects	118

ix Lessons on landscape art

41	The first landscape painting	121
42	Landscapes 'panoramas	123
43	Mixing greens	126
44	Painting snow	129
45	Effects for mist and fog	132
46	Inclement weather	135
47	Reflections in water	138
48	The colour of clouds	141
49	Sunset hues	144
50	Perspectives in buildings	146
51	Historical village scenes	150
52	Stone circles	153

x Lessons on alfresco oil painting

53	Alfresco painting groundwork part 1: what to bring	156
54	Alfresco painting groundwork part 2: The homemade pochade box	160
55	The first plein air painting	163
56	Painting in a public place	166

xi Lessons on life painting

57	Flesh tones	168
58	Proportions of the human figure	171
59	Painting figures from a photograph	174
60	Painting the first portrait	176
61	Painting the model from life	179
62	Painting wildlife in sgraffito	181
63	Glazing technique for animal portraiture	183
64	Organic patterns in nature	186

xii Lessons for further exploration

65	Painting symmetry	188
66	Synthesising art	191
67	Introduction to abstract painting	193
68	The golden section	196

xiii End of course preparation and assessment

69	Setting written assignments	198
70	Presenting artwork	201
71	Photographing paintings	203
72	Varnishing the oil paintings	205
73	Preparing the summative assessment	207
74	The summative assessment	209
75	The purpose of evaluation	211

xiv After-matter

Health and safety for art classes	213
Glossary	216
Suggested Further reading and resources	219
About the author	220

Introduction

The art teacher seldom knows the nature of the art group that is going to materialise on the first session of an oil painting course. The reasons for enrolling may be many and varied: to practice a leisure activity; to meet people with similar interests; to produce paintings for an exhibition; to enhance a job prospect; to augment a course in the visual arts or simply to improve colour mixing skills. Similarly there is no demographic or type. The backgrounds, beliefs and race of each student may and often do, differ.

For this reason, the needs of each student, whether this is domestic, physical or in art ability will vary and could well leave the teacher wondering how a logical scheme of work can be devised. Inevitably, the role of the teacher will be diverse: counsellor, negotiator, manager, adviser, organiser, confidant, appeaser and troubleshooter, stretching the teacher's interpersonal skills as well as teaching skills to the limit. This is why an art course that is coherent, realistic and fulfils the needs of every student is vital within any art course.

This book offers advice for any teacher wishing to deliver a series of lessons on oil painting in post compulsory education. Preparatory chapters on managing a class, building confidence in the students and enforcing inclusive learning can be found within section 2 of this book. Relevant learning theories to enhance teaching skills and to raise awareness of how each student learns serve to help the teacher plan activities to suit every student. Preparing for art class by such means can be found in section 3.

An in depth section on the art materials required for oil painting, such as the mediums, brushes, as well as practical issues of transporting the oil paintings can be found in section 1. A guide on health and safety can be found in section 14 at the back of this book.

The remainder of this book (sections 4 to 12) offers approximately 50 lesson plan ideas for oil painting, including objectives, resources, differentiation and main art activities. Sections are broken down into colour theory, oil painting techniques, still life art, landscape art, figure painting, painting alfresco and challenging lessons for gifted students. Section 13 is dedicated to end-of-course preparation, assessment and evaluation. The teacher may mix up the lesson plan ideas or modify them as required to create a logical scheme of work that will fit a brief.

Please note, the images featured do not necessarily represent what the students should aim for, but serve to give the teacher an idea of what the lesson is supposed to inform.

This, being the black and white version of this title, means it can be produced at a lower price without taking away what is being conveyed within. However, the colour version of this book is available to serve preference.

I Guide to Art Materials

1. Art Materials Needed for Oil Painting

The student who wishes to begin art class will need guidance on what to buy in terms of oil painting materials and outlets that offer value for money. Supplying a product list for art students will help provide an even footing when the painting classes begin. The following informs on the essential art materials associated with oils. The teacher may then distil a shopping list for students.

Types of Oil Paints

Well-established manufacturers of oil paint such as Daler-Rowney and Winsor & Newton provide traditional oil paints in two grades:

Artist Quality Oil Paints: These paints are designed for professionals and contain organic pigments. They are therefore quite costly.

Student Quality Oil Paints: Are the cheaper alternative, as the pigments are made from synthetic sources, yet retain much of the exacting standards of the artist quality paints. Student quality oils are perfectly suited to the practicing student and I myself have used them extensively.

Artisan Watersoluble Oil Paint: is an alternative to traditional oils for those who are allergic to substances such as solvents. Artisan also simplifies the associated materials, as only water is required to thin the paint, although a range of equivalent mediums to suit watersoluble oils, such as linseed oil, can be found.

Alkyd Oils: Although not really oil paint and is therefore a misnomer, alkyds deserve a mention here, as they have similar properties to oil paint mixed with alkyd medium. Alkyds are essentially pigment suspended in a specially-modified resin that provides a quick-drying paint layer, ideal for applying glazes (thin layers of paint).

Essential Oil Pigments

Some artists get by with just three primary colours and white for oil sketches. Others like to have a multitude of pigments. But lots of oil colours are not essential. Similarly, the purchase of a set of tubes should be avoided, as they could contain redundant colours such as orange or cream which can easily be achieved by mixing essential colours. This is why buying tubes singly is recommended.

The primary colours are a vital inclusion to any colour arsenal, but not any red, yellow and blue is necessarily a primary colour as impurities often exist within. Ultramarine, for instance contains a lot of violet. Primary colours are explored more fully in section 6, but for now, the colours that resemble the primaries of printing ink, magenta, yellow and cyan, will produce clean mixes. In terms of oil pigments, these might be denoted by the word "process" or "Winsor" on the label, such as "process blue." I have found pthalo blue, permanent rose and cadmium yellow (pale) pretty close to the true primary colours and have recommended them widely.

The following set of pigments therefore will produce just about any mix the students need: titanium white, permanent rose, cadmium red, lemon yellow, cadmium yellow (pale), pthalo blue, ultramarine, viridian, burnt sienna and burnt umber. Students, of course may wish to add other colours to their collection.

Pigments are available in many tube sizes, but a set of pigments of 37 or 38ml with a 100ml tube of titanium, will cover dozens of medium-sized canvases or art boards and are easy to transport.

Art Brushes

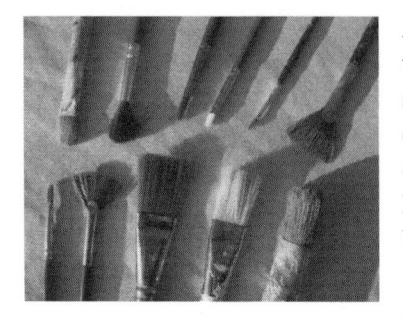

A vast collection of oil brushes is unnecessary for oil painting. The student may start with a small collection and build up gradually once familiar with personal needs. Really, there are only two types of brushes for oil painting.

Soft brushes: for detail and blending. Soft brushes are usually made from the sable or a blend of sable and synthetic hair. Acrylic brushes can also be used for oils, but take care not to purchase watercolour brushes as they lack the springiness required to handle the heavy properties of the oil paint.

Stiff brushes: for impasto and large areas of paint. These brushes are usually made from ox hair or similar stiff bristle. The ends of the bristles are split into "flags" which enables the brush to hold more paint. Household brushes from a DIY store would be suitable but cheap brands that moult onto the painting should be avoided.

Both brush types come in different shapes which are:

- Round brush: These brushes taper to a point and are designed for applying detail such as hair or twigs.
- Rigger: These are like the round brush, but the bristles are much longer. This brush was originally intended for applying detail to the rigging of ships hence the name.
- Flat, otherwise known as bright: These brushes end bluntly for the application of thick strokes of paint.
- Filbert: these brushes possess a blunt end like the flat, but the overall shape is more rounded for soft strokes.
- Fan brush: The bristles fan out and are therefore ideal for the application of thin washes and for soft blending.

All brush shapes are sold in sizes denoted by numbers; the higher the number the larger the brush.

The following brush sizes of both types will come in useful within a beginner's kit.

- Sizes 3 and 6 round sables for fine detail. Riggers may be incorporated.
- Sizes 6 and 10 bright or filbert sables for soft blending. A fan brush may alternatively be used.
- Sizes 6 and 10 bright or filbert hog or substitute bristle for rough brushwork such as skies.
- A large bright or filbert hog or similar for the application of large areas of paint such as backgrounds or glazes.

Care of the Brushes

The lifespan of oil brushes can be prolonged with care. After the end of each painting session, lather the bristles right up to the ferrule (the metal banding that holds the bristles in place) in soap or neat washing up liquid. Rinse off in warm water. Repeat until all traces of paint is gone. Press the bristle back into shape with a little Vaseline and store pointing upwards in a jar to retain their shape.

Other mark-making implements such as palette knives, old combs, sponges and toothbrushes can be used for scratching, scumbling or sgraffito techniques.

A Disposable Mixing Palette

Any non-porous material can be used as an artist's palette. An old china plate, a plastic sheet or laminated wood would be ideal. For convenience cling-film can be tensioned over a piece of wood via bulldog clips. Once finished with, the cling-film can be folded inwards to be disposed of without having to clean the palette after the lesson.

Artists' Mediums

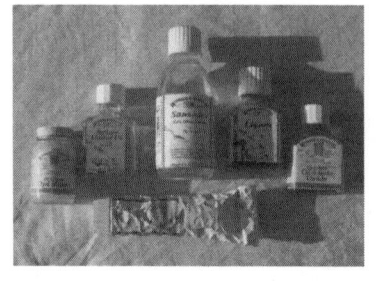

Oil paint can be modified with various agents known as mediums.

The most essential medium is artist solvent which thins the oil paint into washes and cleans the brushes. Household solvents or turps must never be used as they are harsh to the brushes and emit powerful odours. Low-odour artist white spirit such as Sansador or Turpenoid is much more preferable. Artist solvents can last longer by leaving used solvent to stand until the paint settles to the bottom. Pour off the clean solution into another jar to be reused.

Solvents excepted, there are two types of oil painting mediums: oil-based mediums and alkyd-based mediums.

Oil-based mediums are simply oils derived from organic matter such as seeds, most notably linseed. Organic oils are added to the oil paint to increase transparency, flow and to retard the paint's drying time. The application of a thin layer of paint is known as a "glaze." Linseed oil is the most popular choice for such an application, although sunflower oil can be used for pale colours as it is non-yellowing.

Alkyd-based mediums are formulated from a synthetic resin that will accelerate the drying time of the oil paint. Liquin is the alkyd's answer to linseed oil. It will increase the flow and transparency of the oil paint for glazing techniques, but it will not leave a glossy appearance and has the advantage of drying quickly for rapid applications of glazes.

Impasto medium will add body to the paint for impasto techniques. Do not be put off by its brown appearance. Once the gel has been mixed with the pigment, it will not affect its hue.

Linseed oil is a useful medium for beginners and is used most widely. With practice and confidence, students may wish to experiment with other mediums such as impasto medium or Liquin.

Surfaces for Oil Painting

The practice of oil painting is traditionally associated with canvasses. However, other surfaces are perfectly suited to oil painting and are cheaper. Such a surface is known as a "support." Wood, card, stretched linen and even watercolour paper can be used as a support if properly sealed. Such a sealant is known as a "ground" or "size" which protects the support from the degrading effects of the oil in the paint. Preparing your own art surfaces will save lots of money on purchasing ready-prepared art surfaces. More about preparing your own in a moment.

Ready Prepared Art Surfaces

Students who wish to get on with the business of painting may purchase ready-prepared art surfaces from specialist outlets, hobby shops or even supermarkets.

Stretched canvases can be found in fine, medium and coarse grain. Fine grain is suitable for detailed paintings; coarse grain for expressive paintings. Avoid box canvases, as their depth take up lots of storage and adds unnecessary bulk.

The large outlet, Daler Rowney famously stock Daler boards, a popular choice for it offers a firmer surface for painting and similarly can be found in different textures. Daler boards are simply ready-primed thick card. Some consist of primed linen-canvas stretched and glued onto board. Other art manufacturers supply similar art boards for oil painting which might offer value for money. Old used art boards may be primed over and used again if necessary.

Oil Painting Sketch Pads

Oil painting paper can be found in pads, like sketch pads only the paper has been specially-prepared for oil painting. Different textures can be found to emulate real canvas. Such pads usually come in sets of twelve.

Gessoes for Oil Painting

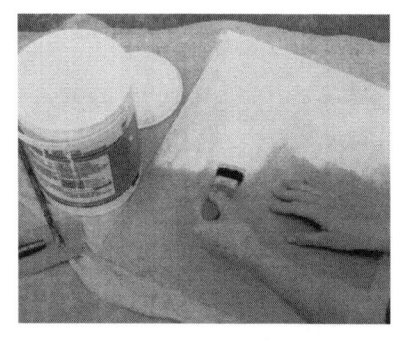

Preparing your own art surfaces for oil painting drastically cuts cost and is not time consuming. The artist is also given control over the surface on which to paint. The only other purchase required is a gesso.

Gessoes, grounds, sizes and sealants in oil painting terms are really one and the same: an agent that prevents the oil in the paint from sinking into the support, causing the oil to rot the material. Several types are available on the market. For informative purposes, the main types are:

Traditional Gesso

This is the oldest type of sealant. Gesso is chalk or whiting suspended in a glue binding agent, usually rabbit skin glue. The glue is applied onto the support first. This is called "sizing." The gesso mixture is then applied on top.

Oil-Based Primer

This type of primer offers a smoother and glossier finish. Again, a coat of size is required before the oil-based primer can be applied. Being oil-based, the paint takes a day or so to dry and the brushes must be cleaned in solvents afterwards.

Preparing your Own Art Surfaces with Acrylic Polymer Primer

Acrylic primer is the easiest to use and the one I would most recommend. Also known as "acrylic gesso primer," this sealant is simply an acrylic-based paint that is water-based and quick-drying. Once dry, it is water resistant, tough and provides the ideal surface onto which to apply the oil paint. Brushes merely need washing in warm soapy water afterwards.

If applying acrylic primer onto wood panel such as MDF or hardboard, lightly sand with fine glass-paper first to provide a key. Apply the primer with a wide brush, moving in all directions and brushing out ridges. Once dry, sand the surface again if necessary for extra smoothness.

Watercolour Paper for Oil Painting

Watercolour paper is ideal for oil painting as it is thick and comes in various textures. "Not" paper has a random texture as it has been "cold pressed," which means that heat has not been involved in the pressing. "Hot pressed" or HP watercolour paper has a smoother texture and is ideal for detailed work. 300 gsm or thicker is best. Good quality card, such as mount-board can also be used.

To prime card or paper, clip or tape a sheet onto backing board. Apply the primer with a soft, wide brush. Don't worry too much if the paper buckles a little. It will flatten out once dry. When the primer is dry, apply a second coat. Leave the clips in place until the primer is completely dry.

Lightweight Easels

Whether to purchase an easel or not is up to the student, but in many cases, an easel is not really necessary. A drawing-board with bulldog clips to hold the painting in place might serve just as well and is compact.

However, table easels might offer a little more convenience. The table easel, as the name suggests, sits on a raised surface and provides an angled support where the painting rests. The student may complete the painting whilst sitting at a table or desk, rather like a draughtsman. Compartments are sometimes available for the storage of art materials.

For informative purposes, other types of easels can be purchased or hired. Free standing easels are suitable for the artist who prefers to stand and paint, as when life painting. French easels are lightweight for mobility and fold compactly.

Studio Easels

The tripod or A-frame studio easel is a sturdier alternative, and its ratchet mechanism enables flexibility in the painting's height and angle adjustment. The art student who wishes to undertake a series of large works exceeding four feet on any side may find the H-frame studio easel most suitable. The H-frame easel, the ultimate in sturdiness is really designed to be a permanent fixture within the studio for its size and weight and can be found in most art colleges.

Whichever the students opts for, carrying issues must be taken into account.

Pochade Boxes

Pochade boxes, or artists' cigar boxes, as they are sometimes called, are the most compact contraption. These are small carry boxes with an angled lid, rather like a laptop. The ultimate gadget for the mobile artist, the pochade box provides storage for the art materials and a slotted compartment where the wet painting may be stored without fear of it getting ruined during transit. A guide on how to make your own carrier for wet oil paintings, particularly for painting *en plein air*, can be found in chapter 54, which will help students to save money.

Other Oil Painting Materials

The following might come in useful for the art student.

- An art bin or toolbox with tiered drawers to store the materials.
- Pots.
- Rags.
- Pencils, eraser, ruler and scalpel.
- An artist's viewfinder (see chapter 19).
- Acrylic paints in the colours burnt sienna, white, red, yellow and blue may come in useful for applying a quick-drying underwash for an oil painting. Acrylics are cheap, quick drying, watersoluble paints that dry water resistant. Brushes must be cleaned in water immediately afterwards.

Essential Oil Painting Materials

The art student need not purchase all the art materials mentioned to begin oil painting. In fact, effective oil paintings can be produced with just seven oil colours, two brushes, art solvent and primed paper. The art teacher however may set out a list of the most essential art materials required for the class, using this chapter as a guide. The students can then make informed decisions on what to bring prior to art instruction.

II Students' Needs

2. Multi-Sensory Art Lesson Planning

A teacher expounding at length on colour theory front of a whiteboard is unlikely to fulfil everybody's learning needs and may result in a fidgety art class. This is because every student has a preference in how the information is presented, lesson to lesson, moment to moment and even according to mood. Such preferences are known as learning styles.

What are Learning Styles?

Everyone processes information through three different channels, also known as the VAK model, which stands for visual, auditory and kinaesthetic.

- Visual. This is learning through the eyes. This entails the use of diagrams, such as colour wheels, paintings, watching demonstration, colour mixing, judging tones and composing a painting.
- Auditory. This is learning through the ears. This entails listening and hearing, such as heeding instructions, listening to lectures, taking part in brain storming sessions and participating in discussions.
- Kinaesthetic. This is learning through touch and feel. This entails applying the paint with the fingers, smudging paint, sgraffito or impasto techniques.

Visual preferences

It could be argued that individuals who are drawn to painting will have a strong visual preference. However, a comprehensive learning experience will involve all three channels to create a multi-sensory lesson plan. This means breaking the lesson up into different activities and mixing it up. A well-rounded art lesson might begin with a short presentation on colour theory and the definition of complementary colours, which will fulfil the auditory channels. This might be followed by a demonstration on how to mix complementary colours to achieve progressively darker hues. This will fulfil the visual channels. The students may then explore colour behaviour for themselves. This will satisfy the kinaesthetic channels.

The results of the colour mixing exercise might be assessed and evaluated via a group discussion, relating individual's experiences and ways that colour mixing technique might be improved or developed. The lesson might conclude with a short question and answer session, reinforcing what has been learned so far. Auditory and visual channels are revisited.

As can be seen, the lesson plan could include various types of activities that engage the senses via different channels.

A Multi-sensory Art Lesson

But not every art lesson needs to progress in this way. Some lessons may be "quieter" than others, and indeed, students may sometimes prefer to be left to complete a project without interruption. But using the VAK model to best effect throughout a series of painting lessons, are more likely to help students complete the course having learned something about painting and in a way that stimulate students' interest.

3. The Individual Learning Plan and Differentiation

An individual learning plan, or ILP, is a personalised and flexible route where a learner may achieve a given goal. An ILP may need to be drawn up if a student has a particular issue with drawing, painting or other special need that impacts upon the learning experience. The ILP makes the art lesson inclusive for all the learners. Creating such flexibility is known as "differentiation."

When an ILP is Needed

An initial assessment (explained in chapter 7) will highlight any such areas that may need special attention. Examples of situations where an ILP is needed might be:

- If a student has a particular difficulty grasping perspectives or shading technique.
- If a student has a lengthy journey to the lesson, or domestic commitments, that impact upon the time spent painting.
- If a special needs impacts upon the learning experience, such as poor hearing or poor hand coordination. In such cases, a learning mentor may be assigned.

Drawing up an ILP

The ILP must be agreed between the teacher, the student and (if applicable) the learning mentor so that the student fully understands what is expected. Copies should be kept by all parties for future reference.

The ILP must contain clear, precise and measurable objectives that can easily be assessed. This is known as SMART objectives, discussed in more depth in chapter 10; the mnemonic stands for (and which is reiterated where applicable): specific, measurable, attainable, realistic and time-bound. The goals must be small and progressive. If the student finds a particular objective difficult, it can be subdivided again until such time the full objective has been achieved.

An example of an ILP for a student who has poor understanding of perspectives, for example, might be:

- To copy an idealized cube from a given resource.
- To draw a cuboid object from life, using simple lines.
- To map the vanishing point for the cube.
- To draw a cuboid object from life including the vanishing point.
- To draw a series of objects consisting of perpendicular sides, such as cereal boxes, die or biscuit tins using simple lines.
- To draw a chosen cuboid object from various angles, including head-on, from the side and from above.

Each objective may be tackled during extra time in class, varying between ten minutes and half an hour. Extra attention may be given for the student and assessed where necessary.

An ILP for a student who has a different kind of need, such as a lengthy car journey, causing lateness might be allocated extra time to catch up at home or a time extension to complete a project.

The Learning Mentor

Students who experience barriers with learning may require a learning mentor, although one is not compulsory. In context of the art lesson, the learning mentor may assist the student with domestic tasks, such as comprehension (if the student has learning needs) or with mixing colours (if the student has poor motor skills.) The learning mentor must be involved with deciding the ILP.

4. Motivating Art Students

Classroom management includes motivating students in art lessons otherwise the students may not reach their creative potential.

According to Reece & Walker's book *Teaching, Training and Learning – a Practical Guide* (Business Education Publishers: 2004) a student of low ability but high motivation can experience greater success than a student of high ability and low motivation. For this reason, motivational issues should be treated with equal gravity as a learning need or a disability.

The Causes of Low Motivation

Before tackling this problem, the causes of low motivation in the art class must be identified. The following might be worth exploring:

- The learning environment looks unwelcoming or uncared for. Paint spills and dirty pots full of unusable art brushes can be visually off-putting.
- There is insufficient differentiation in the lesson plan to accommodate those who have a natural flair for drawing and those who might cringe at the idea of drawing a line.
- The learning objectives are unclear, leaving students unsure of what is expected of them.
- SMART objectives (see chapter 10) have not been applied.
- Basic human needs have not been addressed, leaving issues such as tiredness, hunger, physical discomfort and stress to hamper creative expression.
- Unchecked disruption in class hindering the focus required for completing a painting or drawing.

Although there might be limitations on what a teacher can do, the following alterations might enhance learning experience.

Displaying the students' work on the walls shows their creations are valued. Altering the display periodically will refresh the view and provide a talking point. A tidy environment free of clutter will create a more welcoming and cared for atmosphere.

Adjusting the differentiation in the lesson plans in order to accommodate those who enjoy a challenge as well as those who have little confidence in painting. This will ensure both will experience success in learning and provide opportunities for praise. This may involve blending both the cognitive and the behaviourist approach to teaching (see chapter 11).

Ensuring objectives are clear and achievable. This will help students feel secure in what is expected of them (see chapter 10).

Identifying issues and finding solutions to problems such as tiredness in the evenings or hunger near lunchtime will help art students focus on the task at hand.

Praise in Art Class

Last, but not least, praising has fundamental effect upon motivation. The student for instance who finds it hard to draw a straight line will feel liberated by small achievements, as well as the more able student who has been stretched creatively. Finding any opportunity to praise will often compel the student to venture further.

Stimulating Creative Processes

The causes of low motivation in art class must be identified before they can be tackled effectively. Improving the art environment may help creativity as well as outlining clear and visible objectives. Differentiating the lesson plan to accommodate students' diverse drawing and painting abilities is likely to providing opportunities for success and praise – a key point. Chapter 75 explores problem solving by evaluation and employing the reflective cycle.

5. Encouraging the Reluctant Art Student

The classroom occasionally contains at least one student who freezes at the thought of depositing paint to paper. Sadly the initial assessment does not always pick up on such issues until the practical exercises ensue. As is the case with painting, identifying the cause will help find a solution and which may in turn nurture student motivation.

Building Confidence in Painting

There are many causes for a reluctance to painting. These might be:

- Beginner's nerves if this if the first time.
- Fear of making mistakes.
- Inability to tap into the inner child that enjoys exploration.
- Low self-esteem.

Sensitivity must be applied. In certain situations, the student might be willing to discuss the causes of this creative block. An overbearing inner critic or anxiety over domestic or financial issues might be hampering freedom of expression. But singling out the student in any way must be avoided. Giving assurance to the student that this affliction is common might ease the situation. In order to develop as a visual artist, the student must be encouraged to apply self-lenience whilst exploring a new art medium. Happy accidents are part of learning, and subduing the inner critic will often open up the creative channels.

Completing a Painting

The following teaching strategies might be applied when encouraging a reluctant student to complete a painting.

- Agree on an individual learning plan with the learner that sets out clear and precise goals (see chapter 3).

- Ensure the goals are small and manageable.
- Ensure the goals provide opportunities for the learner to experience success.
- Use cheap materials during the experimentation to minimise concerns over wasting art materials.

Small Goals and Praise

Small, achievable goals are key to helping the student break the cycle. Examples of such goals might be:

- To apply exploratory marks over the page via different brushes and implements.
- To draw around the stencils at random places on the painting surface and then to filling in the enclosed spaces with a solid colour.
- To mix and apply different colour combinations.
- To apply a contrasting solid colour into a neighbouring stencil shape.
- To lighten a colour by adding small increments of white.
- To darken a colour by adding small increments of a complementary colour.

These goals may be subdivided again into smaller goals if necessary. The aim of simply depositing paint to paper might be all that is required in the first instance. The exercises in chapters 17 and 18 may be incorporated into the lesson plan.

Picking up a Paintbrush

Embarking a painting can be a daunting prospect for some learners who have issues with confidence. The teacher must treat this problem sensitively. Appropriate use of encouragement and praise, as well as an ILP that describes specific and small goals will help the student make the vital transition into painting.

6. Students with Special Needs

Inclusive learning means ensuring that every student is able to take part in painting activities, regardless of ability. But special needs may take many forms: poor motor skills, learning difficulties or a hearing impairment. A learning mentor may be assigned to such a student, but one is not obligatory.

In such cases, the teacher must try to differentiate the lesson plan to include the needs of the learner. The initial assessment will highlight such issues and an individual learning plan (see chapter 3) may need to be agreed.

Inclusive Art Lessons

In the meantime, the teacher can make adjustments to the lesson in order to make the activities suitable to all students, but to take care that special provisions do not impact upon the other learners. Such things might be:

- Setting up the art materials for the special needs student prior to the lesson.
- If the student has lost use of an arm, affixing the painting onto the table to stop it slipping around.
- Allowing the student to sit close to a doorway for convenience.
- Allowing the student to sit at the front if hard of hearing.
- Assisting with mixing colours and cleaning the brushes if time is an issue.

Lesson Plans for Special Needs

It is not always the case, but a student who has such a need may have low self-belief in artistic abilities. In such cases, the tutor may have to think up strategies to help the student overcome mental barriers and to make creative progress within the lesson. The previous three chapters may be referred to.

Definition of Creativity

Of course, the special need rarely has any relevance to artistic ability. A student with Asperger syndrome may have a natural flair for drawing or colour judgment. It so often happens that a "special needs" student requires no support whatsoever during the painting lesson, but may require assistance within other circumstances or other learning environments.

III Preparing to Teach Art

7. The Initial Assessment for Lesson Planning

Before the art teacher can formulate a scheme of work, an initial assessment of the students must be conducted. This makes it possible to tailor lesson plans to fit each student's learning profile and personal aims.

Types of Assessments

Different types of assessments exist. Formative assessments enable students (and the teacher) to check that learning has taken place as the course progresses; this might come in the form of quizzes, practical exercises, discussions, tutorials and painting.

Summative assessments occur at the end of the course, and come in the form of a test under a governing body. The initial assessment, the focus of this chapter, serves to establish where the students are "at" prior to the course.

An Art Course that Fits

An initial assessment is necessary for several reasons. Most importantly, the results can be used to ensure the student is on the correct and most fitting oil painting course. It would be pointless to enroll a student who has higher diploma in art on a course on painting for beginners. Similarly, a student who wishes to improve landscape painting may experience inconvenience if the course was found to be on life drawing.

The initial assessment also enables the teacher to measure the student's progress. A "before" and "after" comparison can then be made at the end of the course that will inform the teacher (and the student) of the student's artistic development.

ILP or Not

With the above satisfied, the art teacher must still initially assess the students to fine-tune the lesson plans and ensure all needs are met. Individual learning plans (or ILPs, explained in chapter 3) are often necessary for students who require special attention, such as those who have a particular difficulty with grasping perspectives. Students with special needs that impact upon the learning may also need an ILP.

Making lessons flexible and inclusive in class is known as "differentiation." This means making art activities adjustable to fit different abilities. For example, an exercise in colour mixing can be made to challenge able students who wish to explore colour behaviour by applying them via advanced techniques. Less able students will also be able to take part by mixing different colour combinations and recording the results. An example of such an exercise can be found in chapter 24.

Assessing Art Students

All students have individual learning profiles when it comes to art. Some students may have a natural gift for drawing, but find applying paint difficult. Other students may have lots of creative ideas, but has no knowledge of art mediums.

On the first evening, the teacher may try to identify each student's strengths, weaknesses, previous learning, special needs and personal objectives. The following form a typical example of a student's initial assessment prior to beginning an art course.

Example of an Initial Assessment

- Name: Student X
- Previous learning: Completed BTEC National Diploma in art. Part completed her degree in Bristol.
- Outline: Interested in textures. She has designed and painted backdrops for her local playgroup. She is familiar with oils, but has few paintings to show for.
- Strengths/weaknesses: Has good colour mixing skills, but perceives her drawing to be particularly weak.
- Personal objective: to improve drawing skills to enhance her degree result. To also complete more paintings for her portfolio.

The results of this particular initial assessment highlight a possible need for an ILP in drawing. Addressing distorted perception in drawing (chapters 15 and 16) might be a start. Previous learning has conversely demonstrated abilities in other areas. A background in theatre design might warrant exploratory artwork incorporating textures. Lesson plans on colour theory, basic drawing technique, composing paintings and using different mediums might be the best course of action.

Initial Assessment in Art

Before the art teacher can formulate a series of lessons in painting, the students must be initially assessed. This ensures each student is on the correct course. With this satisfied, the teacher may establish each student's strengths, weaknesses, special needs and personal objective. The results will help the teacher decide whether ILPs are needed, and to select the most suitable art activities to include within the scheme of work. This is discussed next.

8. The Scheme of Work for Oil Painting

The fledgling art teacher will at some point be faced with the prospect of planning a series of lessons on painting (also called a scheme of work). A theme (see chapter 9) may also need to be decided. When one considers that there are overwhelming topics on the subject, from the art materials required, the techniques involved to the different genres of art, it might be little wonder that the teacher could feel overwhelmed. However, this problem can be overcome by using David Ausubel's Subsumption Theory.

Ausubel's Subsumption Theory for Art

David Ausubel was a cognitivist who believed that in order to learn effectively, individuals must be presented with information in a logical and hierarchical order from the simple to the complex. The lesson plans must reflect this principle by starting with the shortest and easiest tasks, progressing to the more difficult. Attaching new information to the old also makes the new information meaningful and easier to remember. Assimilation can be achieved when information overlaps one another in a fashion that can finally be appreciated holistically. Advanced signposting, consolidation and reinforcement are also used as learning "triggers, enabling students to remember information and utilise what they have learned for future art activities.

Teaching Oil Painting Logically

Bearing in mind these principles, a programme of study for beginners in oil painting, might begin in session 1 (see chapter 13) with an introduction to the course, an initial assessment and perhaps an icebreaker. The following sessions might follow thus:

- Session 2: Introduction to oil paints. What are oils?
- Session 3: Mark-making and exploration with oils.
- Session 4: Colour theory and colour behaviour.

- Session 5: Painting patterns with solid colour.
- Session 6: Light and shadow.
- Session 7: Painting a piece of fruit in oils.
- Session 8: Glazing technique by using linseed oil.
- Session 9: Using impasto medium on a still life study.
- Session 10: Consolidation and final assessment.

Organising an Art Module

The lessons themselves may reflect Ausubel's theory insomuch as:

- The lessons must follow from the simple to the complex.
- The tasks within must begin with the easiest and the shortest to the more difficult and involved.
- The lessons must begin with the familiar and the usual and lead to the unfamiliar and unusual.
- Advanced signposting to the next lesson via informing the students at the end of the lesson on what to expect in the following lesson.
- Plenty of consolidation, recapping and reinforcement.
- Information overlaps one another.
- Attaching new information to old makes it more meaningful.

Coherent Art Classes

Ausubel's Subsumption Theory is a good way of devising a sequence of art lessons. This involves starting from the simple, such as experimentation with mark making, to the complex, such as advanced techniques with oils. Overlapping and recapping on information will help students assimilate what they have learned. A lesson on colours' tonal values, for instance can easily be revisited when painting a still life study. Advanced signposting by informing students on what to expect the next lesson serves to link the lessons together in a coherent fashion.

9. Selecting a Theme for the Course

Formulating a scheme of work is only part of the picture. The teacher may devise an overall theme for the course, which works to hold the lessons together and gives it meaning. The theme, also known as a brief, might be decided by the art institution's curriculum, the teacher, or (if the course allows) the students individually.

Which Theme

The theme serves to give students inspiration or a direction to pursue. The theme should not be too narrow, giving little leeway yet not too broad or vague. The following ideas might give the teacher some idea of what to use as a theme for an art course:

- The colour red.
- Symmetry.
- Patterns in nature.
- Manmade objects.
- Childhood memories.
- Close-ups.

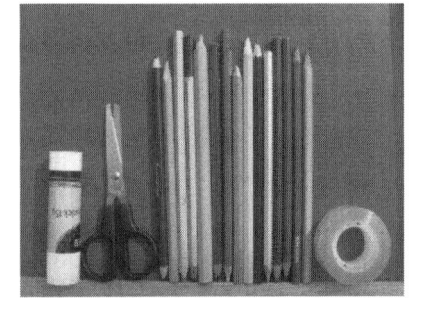

Writing a Brief

Writing a brief for students to explore requires careful thought. The brief should be to the point, offering the following information:

- The theme itself, including suggestions for inspiration.
- Artistic requirements for the summative assessment.
- Written assignments or presentations.
- Assessment date.

The following page shows an example of what a brief looks like. The teacher may talk through the brief with the students on the first lesson.

The Brief: Close-ups

Take a look at an everyday form, such as a tea strainer or a cactus through a magnifying glass and suddenly it takes on a bizarre form and becomes unfamiliar. The artist Georgia O'Keefe did so with her close-up studies of flowers. Looking close-up at things creates a different way of looking at things. I would like you to explore how things look close-up. This can be done by sectioning a part of an image and projecting it onto a large drawing surface, by scaling it up, or simply by taking photos through a magnifying glass.

I would like you to explore the contours, tones, colours and patterns of your chosen objects. Take things a stage further by using the contours to create a repeat pattern or by altering the colours to give it a different context. The final painting does not have to resemble the original object.

Ideas to get you going

- Close-up of dead leaves or other organic matter, such as flowers.
- Close-up of animals or sections of it, so that only an eye or part of the antlers can be seen, for example.
- Close-ups of inanimate objects.
- Close-ups of textures such as wool or sandpaper.
- Other unusual objects.

Creative requirements

1. 1 X sketchbook showing log of creative evidence
2. 1 X A3 experimental work
3. 2 X A3 developmental work
4. 1 X A3 visual conclusion
5. Late submissions and/or a 20% (or greater) absence will impact upon the final marking.

Assessment Date: 23.5.12

The Best Brief

The brief provides inspiration or a direction for art students to pursue within an art course. Students are free to interpret the brief as they wish, whether the work is abstract, representational or other. However, the criteria should be the same for all students in respect of what should be submitted for the summative assessment including what may detrimentally affect the assessment marking. Setting written assignments and deciding the assessment criteria are explained fully in chapters 69 and 74 respectively.

10. Writing Objectives for Art Lessons

Planning art classes entails writing clear objectives that are achievable by the art group. But how does the art teacher write objectives properly?

Oil painting encompasses various approaches and applications: abstract art, landscape painting, still life and exploratory art. Similarly, the class may comprise students of various backgrounds, artistic styles and abilities. The results of the initial assessment, covered in chapter 7 will inform the art teacher and can be used to formulate the most suitable art objectives for the group.

Difference between Aims and Objectives

Students will embark upon an art class with various aspirations and hopes. These might be to improve colour mixing, to develop a portfolio for an art course or to find original ideas for painting. These generalised statements of intent are known as "aims" or "outcomes", and in teaching context are vitally different to objectives. Aims can be collated to help the teacher formulate a scheme of work for painting, but when it comes to lesson planning, SMART objectives must be precise and demonstrable.

SMART Objectives for Lesson Painting

SMART is a mnemonic that stands for specific, measurable, attainable, realistic and time-bound. This means that each objective cannot be subjective or vague. They must suit the levels of the student, are achievable in the allotted time and can easily be assessed by evidence. A typical art lesson may contain anything from one to four objectives. Examples of art objectives might be:

- To produce a tonal strip by introducing increasing amounts of white paint to a given colour.
- To make a viewfinder.

- To paint a still life consisting of two objects.
- To apply an oil-glaze over an underlying glaze of a conflicting colour.
- To produce a ten minute presentation on the colour theory.

Art Objectives

Objectives must be made to fit each student's individual learning profile as some students will have good ability in colour mixing, yet require development in drawing. Allowing for this differentiation means rewording the objectives to reflect these different abilities; observing the Bloom's Taxonomy model is a good strategy to use.

Classifications of Art Activities

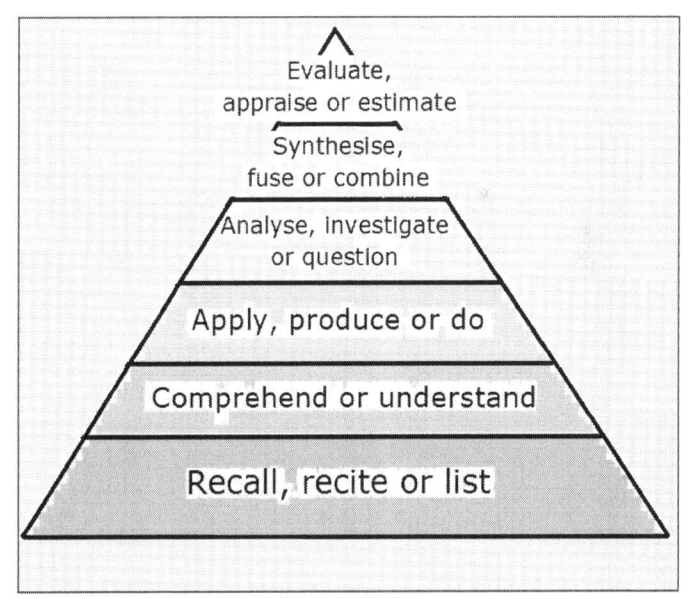

```
            ∧
       Evaluate,
   appraise or estimate
       Synthesise,
     fuse or combine
    Analyse, investigate
        or question
     Apply, produce or do
   Comprehend or understand
     Recall, recite or list
```

Bloom's Taxonomy on Classifications of Thinking.

Benjamin Bloom (1961) conceived classifications of cognitive thought. This is expressed as a pyramid exhibiting six stages of mental development. This pyramid is known as "Taxonomy." The lower levels of thinking must be satisfied before moving onto the next. The diagram shows the six stages.

The verbs used within art objectives can be adjusted to reflect the level of the art class concerned. The objectives just mentioned reflect the third level, as all activities involve "applying" or "producing" (or a synonym). These six levels can be clarified when put into context, as can be seen from the following art objectives.

- Recall: To recall the primary colours of painting.
- Explain: To explain what a primary colour is.
- Apply: To complete an oil painting using only the primary colours.
- Analyse: To examine by discussion why the mixture of two primary colours results in a darker colour.
- Synthesise: To create a new way of mixing primary colours by incorporating another painting method such as glazing or impasto.
- Evaluate: To evaluate by discussion the colour mixing exercise to work out better ways of blending primary colours for painting.

Writing Art Objectives

Utilising Bloom's Taxonomy when planning art activities will enable the teacher to avoid mismatching objectives with the students' abilities – after all, an absolute beginner is unlikely to succeed in evaluating via a ten minute presentation how glazing can best be applied, but might be able to explain what different art mediums do. Success in learning is essential to art planning, and is why targeting art objectives accurately is so crucial.

Evidence of Students' Learning

An important note before closing the subject: care must be taken to avoid using such verbs as "to know" or "to understand," or "to be aware of," within art objectives, even though this forms the second tier of Bloom's pyramid. As mentioned earlier, comprehension must be evidenced in some way, either by writing about it, verbalising it or by applying it in paint. The teacher can then assess student's learning accurately and ensure that the information has indeed sunk in. Appropriate verbs are used within the art objectives throughout this book.

Learning Objectives for Art

Writing art objectives to suit the class means conducting an initial assessment (chapter 7) of the students to ensure they are enrolled upon the correct art course. From this, specific and measureable objectives can be distilled to suit the class and encourage progression. Using Bloom's Taxonomy is a useful tool to help the teacher differentiate each objective so that every student may complete each task as assigned. This will enable them to experience success in learning.

11. Independent Learning in Art Class: Behaviourism versus Cognitivism

Creativity in art class often stems from cognitive thought processes in the students, which can be encouraged by strategic teaching methods.

As discussed earlier, an art class will often contain a medley of students with different needs and art abilities. For this reason, the teacher must blend a diversity of art activities within the lesson plans to fulfil each need. This also applies to *how* the activities are delivered. Some students are likely to need highly-directed lessons; others may prefer subtle guidance, where they are helped to find their own solutions.

Teaching Methods for Art

Two basic teaching approaches may be used to satisfy both approaches. These are cognitivism and behaviourism. The definitions of each are as follows:

Behaviourism is based on the idea, that behaviour can be learned without cognitive thought processes. In context of the art class, the behaviourist model is teacher-directed and dictatorial. This is also known as pedagogy.

Art activities are highly-directed and structured, such as following a step-by-step instruction on applying an oil glaze or darkening the colour yellow by specific degrees. Behaviourism may also be used to manage a class. Clapping the hands to embarrass a student out of texting describes an automatic response with no cognitive thought. Conditioning through punishment or reward is known as "operant conditioning."

Cognitivism, a more humanistic and liberal approach, describes a method that encourages independent thought through critical thinking, reflection, reasoning, analysis and synthesis. The student adopting this approach may ask "why?" which might be to the problem of "why does my still life composition look imbalanced?" or "why does my life drawing have garish colours?" This approach is student-directed and self-directed. Such a teaching method is also known as andragogy.

Parallels can be drawn between the Bloom's Taxonomy model referred to in chapter 10 and the two teaching approaches. The lower three levels of Bloom's Taxonomy reflect the behaviourist view; the upper three layers, reflect the cognitivist view.

When to Use Behaviourism in Art Lessons

A behaviourist-biased art course might be best suited to less able learners or a lively class. Beginners might also feel more secure with prescriptive objectives that are easy to measure. The initial stages of an art course are often dominated with behaviourist activities, where all students begin on a level footing and the teacher directs students and explains matters such as health and safety, the course objectives and class rules. Behaviourism might be appropriate to move the class along if paintings need to be ready for assessment. However, more gifted students might become fidgety if the course is heavily-laden with highly-directed art activities.

Cognitive Art Activities

More able or confident art students may thrive on art activities that encourage cognitive thought. This might be to complete a research assignment into colour theory or to give a presentation informing on the organic sources of oil pigments.

Cognitive art activities might also be used to encourage students to evaluate established painting habits for change and improvement or to explore untried art techniques.

Exclusive use of either cognitive or behavourist art activities is unlikely to promote a healthy atmosphere that encourages creativity in art. Both are needed in various amounts depending upon the situation and the needs of the students. Indeed, the teacher may conceive a mixture of pedagogy and andragogy as required. A beginner, for example, may not be ready to combine two painting techniques or to write a self-directed essay evaluating the finished work but may welcome a highly-directed demonstration on scumbling paint.

Teaching Methods for Art

Artistic inspiration can often be a fickle thing and can easily be quashed if the art class has little structure and no clear objectives, which is why appropriate behaviourist methods in teaching are important. However, the teacher must incorporate some art activities that encourage cognitive thought into the lesson plans. Strategic use of both teaching methods, as well as objectives that reflect the levels of Bloom's Taxonomy, will ensure that the needs of each student are met and also promote a more creative environment.

12. Icebreaker ideas

Icebreakers are games and quizzes that help bring a group together. They are not compulsory but may help break down or minimise potential barriers, which unchecked, may cause certain students to withdraw or feel isolated. Some students may be more willing than others to participate, in which case, the teacher may need to modify the icebreaker activity to suit the group to avoid potential embarrassment or discomfort.

Before embarking upon the activity, the teacher must think about the time factor to ensure it does not impact too much upon the rest of the lesson. The room layout should also be considered; is there enough space for the activity? Does the furniture need to be moved? Do any of the students have special needs that require modifications to the icebreaker, such as handouts for the hard of hearing? The simplest and minimal resources are best; many such games of which require token pens and paper.

The following ideas may spur inspiration.

Art Icebreakers

Truth or lie about an artist: A student writes two truths and a lie about a famous artist. The other students (in teams) must determine the lie and earn points. Each student must take a turn.

Drawing consequences: A group of students must draw part of a face, body or other subject matter on a piece of paper, then fold it over, revealing only the continuation lines for the next student's contribution. An example might be to draw the face, fold over and pass it on, the next student draws the torso and arms, fold over and pass it on, the next student draws the legs, fold over and pass it on. The last student draws the feet. Cartoons, aliens and bizarre representations of the feature are encouraged. Opening out the paper will often exhibit funny and weird creations.

A question of art: Write an open question on the whiteboard, such as: "Subject matter I would most like to paint and why..." or "My most disastrous painting..." or "My favourite subject matter is and why..." or "Painting you would least see me do is and why..." or "Why I began painting..." Students may pick one question and answer in turn.

Art charades: Divide the class into two groups. Each student writes the name of an artist or an art related subject and places it into the group's hat. Hats are swapped. The paper is redistributed to each opposing team. Each student must mime what is written on the paper within one minute. A point is awarded to the team that gets the mime.

Team Games

Of course the icebreaker game does not have to have an art theme, but one which can bring any group together within any context. The following are popular choices for team building:

Magic numbers: break the art group into teams of equal numbers, say, three or four, and ask all members to find a corresponding number of unusual facts they have in common. Ban common themes such as hair colour or birth places.

Guess whose fact: Get each student to write an unusual or interesting fact about him or herself; each piece of paper should be folded and placed into a hat. Mix it up and redistribute. In a circle, the first student may read out a fact and try to guess who the fact belongs to. If the guess is wrong, the piece of paper is passed to the next student and so on until the guess is correct and a point is awarded. The next fact is then read by the next student in the circle.

Paper towers: Using only paper, teams of equal number must try to build the tallest tower within twenty minutes. Various strategies might be used, such as paper folding or bending. No other resources are allowed.

Guess the celebrity: The teacher pins the names of celebrities onto the backs of the students. In pairs, one student must guess the name pinned on his back via five questions, where the answer must only be "yes "or "no."

Art Pictionary: Students must try to convey a subject, person or idea by the use of drawings alone. No symbols or letters are allowed. Each team has alternate goes. Points are scored to the team that guesses the answer in one minute.

Class Bonding Games

There is no shortage of fun games the teacher might conceive, from quizzes to challenges. Such icebreakers can be used to help students get to know each other and create a better group dynamic. Consideration must be given to the size of the room, the resources needed, the time factor and the students' needs.

IV The Initial Lessons

13. The First Painting Class

Objective 1: To induct students to the course.
Objective 2: To practice health and safety.
Objective 3: To practice an icebreaker activity (if applicable).
Objective 4: To record an initial assessment.
Objective 5: To recite the course brief.
Objective 6: To recite resource requirements.
Objective 7: To recite the next lesson's objective.

The initial art class might or might not involve much painting depending upon the time factor and domestic matters to attend to, as can be seen from the class objectives above. The following serve to clarify:

- Class register and necessary paperwork.
- Health and safety. This is covered in section 14 at the end of this book.
- Introduction to the teacher and the course. This might involve a question and answer session, discussion and a rundown of what is covered within the scheme of work.
- The course theme (see chapter 9).
- Information on the art materials and necessary other resources required for the course (see guidance in chapter 1).
- Perhaps an icebreaker session (see chapter 12) to help create a better group dynamic.
- The teacher might decide to conduct an initial assessment of the students (see chapter 7), although this might already be conducted prior to the class.
- The criteria requirements of the summative assessment and factors that may impact upon the final marking (see chapters 73 and 74).

Preliminary Matters

Time taken over the preliminaries will often impact upon the first lesson. For this reason, keeping to a schedule is important. Moving things along might also be necessary if things get bogged down during a question and answer session or the icebreaker. But creating a welcoming atmosphere is most important, maintaining courtesy as well as a willingness to help and answer questions.

Permitting more time than necessary for each activity helps prevent the lesson running behind schedule. Providing handouts on matters of health and safety or a rundown of the art materials required will save time on verbal exposition.

Modifying the Scheme of Work

As mentioned in the introduction, the teacher rarely knows what type of group will materialise on the first evening; the governing body's initial assessment often provides basic (if any) information on the students' abilities or motives for enrolling. For this reason, the teacher may need to modify the course accordingly.

Personally, I will conduct my own initial assessment of each student. Doing so provides a more immediate and clearer picture of each student's needs, art abilities and aspirations. Gleaning students' art portfolios (if supplied) can provide an excellent picture of the students' artistic style. The results may highlight a need for individual learning plans (chapter 3), and also a need to modify the scheme of work. It would be pointless to include a lesson on abstract painting, if it so happens all the students have expressed a wish to explore techniques for realism.

Giving what the Students Want

Some students might be happy to get on with an ongoing project whilst the teacher attends to other matters; other students might need a simple painting exercise to prevent idle hands. Depending upon the students' abilities, taking a line for a walk (chapters 17 and 18) or increments of tones (chapter 21) might be suitable activities.

Alternatively, providing visual resources or still life objects may be necessary; the lesson on reflected light outlined in chapter 34 requires minimal resources and is highly recommended for a first art lesson. The subject matter encourages sensitive observation and can easily be differentiated if different objects are used.

Satisfying Students' Expectations

Students should leave the first art lesson fully informed on what to expect from the course, and also what to bring for the next lesson. Potential problems or questions should be taken into account, answered or resolved. Students should also be able to make informed decisions on whether the course fulfils his or her needs.

14. The Definition of Painting

Objective: To write a one-paragraph summary on the definition of painting.

Key skills initiative means the art teacher may need to incorporate literacy into arts education. Exploring the meaning of painting is one such way.

Students might be stuck for words when asked directly what painting means in context of the visual arts. This is likely due to the diverse forms that painting takes, as well as having different meanings to different people. Crystallising a definition might be the ideal objective for the first art lesson, and is a good way of bringing the art group together.

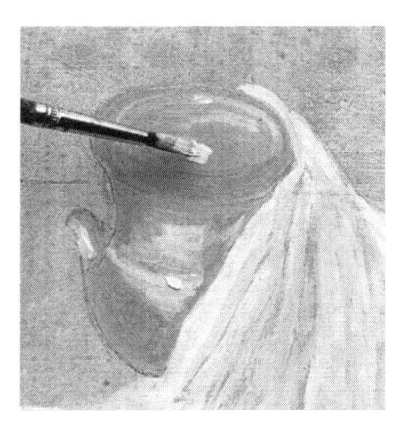

The Meaning of Art

The art lesson might open with a brainstorming session where students might supply snap responses or find the first words that come to mind when asked what painting means. The teacher might then transcribe these words and phrases onto the whiteboard for students to explore. This teaching strategy will help students make contributions to the art class and spur a group discussion, although some students might need prompting.

Thought-shower for Art

Obvious associations are likely to be suggested first, followed by more lateral thinking. Oils, watercolours, art movements, Expressionism, colour theory, Impressionism, Picasso and cave paintings, for instance might be followed by less obvious suggestions, such as colour therapy or chiaroscuro. The aim is for students to express their own personal definitions, to share them, exchange ideas and finally to formulate a definition in their own words.

Painting Classifications

Once the discussion has run its course, the teacher might put forward the definition from an authorative source, such as the Oxford English Dictionary or similar. The following excerpts are from the Cassell Dictionary and Thesaurus *(Cassell: 2004)*.

"Painting: The act, art or occupation of laying on colour or producing representations in colours."

"Art: Creative activity concerned with the production of aesthetic objects or of beauty in general."

Evaluation of what Painting Means

With both the authorative sources and the students' own suggestions, new definitions can be created after reflection. A written assignment can be put forward for the next art lesson. The meaning may be written in one paragraph consisting of two or three sentences that exhibits logical thought. But this task is not as straightforward as it sounds, for every word must count. A thesaurus will be invaluable. Placing this definition in a prominent place within the portfolio might stimulate cognitive thought and keep students focused upon their own personal meanings during the creative process. Such an exercise also enables students to practice literacy in the visual arts.

The written assignment must be easy to assess and not subjective. In this vein, the definition must:

- Be put into the students' own words.
- Be grammatically sound and free of typos.
- Make logical sense.
- And encompass what painting means.

An in depth guide on setting written assignments can be found in chapter 69.

Art Activity Idea

Assigning students the task of writing a personal summary of what painting means to them enables the practice of key skills in the visual arts. Blending a brainstorming session with authorative sources is a good way of stimulating cognitive thought processes and creating new ideas. Keeping these personal meanings handy offers some context when the visual work is viewed and remind students what painting means to them.

V Lessons to Underpin Painting

15. Distorted Perception in Drawing

Objective 1: To visually map aspects of an image as directed by the teacher.

Objective 2: To draw an object from an unfamiliar angle, such as in foreshortening or close-up.

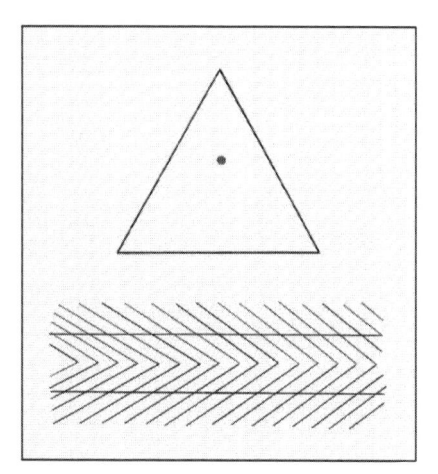

Problems with drawing can often cause problems with the painting. But overcoming such difficulties may lie in an awareness of distorted perception in drawing, which may be caused by an inner dogma regarding how objects look.

Distorted perceptions can manifest itself in various ways in drawing, creating frustration for some students. Common examples of inaccuracies in drawing might be:

- Drawing hands and feet too small in relation to the body.
- Drawing eyes too near to the top of the head because the mind perceives the area above the eyes as less important than the face itself.
- Inaccurate portrayal of foreshortenings (long objects such as fingers, scissors or bottles viewed head-on) because this creates a perceptual dilemma.
- The drawing might look squashed up and tight, or just "wrong."

Making Visual Estimates

The art teacher may begin the drawing lesson by projecting an image of a triangle containing a dot, as shown in the diagram, and to ask the students to judge by eye where the dot is in relation to the top and the bottom of the triangle. This can be done by placing a cross onto a chart. This simple exercise is likely to create a split in opinion and spur a discussion. In most cases, however, the dot will be perceived to be above centre, where in fact, it is dead centre. This can be proved by measuring the position of the dot with a ruler.

Orientation of Lines

A further exercise involves projecting a second image showing two lines intersected by chevrons, as shown below the triangle, and asking the students whether the two lines are perfectly parallel or at an angle to one another. The results for most are likely to be that the lines are not parallel to one another. In fact, the two lines are perfectly parallel.

Reality versus Perception

The objective of the two exercises is to demonstrate that what is perceived by the brain is not always accurate and may interfere with drawing ability. Distorted perception is the mind's tendency to edit and distort reality in a bid to make sense of the world. This may mean applying prescriptive labels and descriptions for objects.

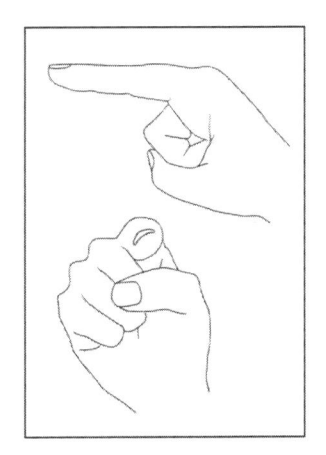

Drawing objects in foreshortening may demonstrate distorted perception at its worst.

Drawing Exercise

The students may explore how the brain

55

distorts reality by completing two simple line-drawings of the hand with one finger extended as though pointing. The first drawing must depict the hand pointing to the side, the second, pointing towards the eye as shown in the diagram. It is likely that the first drawing will be much easier to complete than the second because the second contains a foreshortening effect, which creates a perceptual dilemma. When the exercise is complete, the students may self-evaluate and compare each other's drawing experiences. This will spur a discussion on why the second exercise was more difficult than the first.

Students may continue to practice drawing objects in unfamiliar angles such as foreshortening, close-up or upside down, as these simple exercises helps switch off the part of the brain that makes assumptions about how objects "should" look. Other objects of varying complexities can be drawn from unfamiliar angles to suit ability, such as clothes pegs, bottles, scissors or tin openers.

A lesson exploring foreshortenings in still life can be found in chapter 37.

16. Ways to Improve Drawing

Objective: To complete a simple line drawing by specific methods as instructed by the teacher.

Some students appear to have a natural flair for drawing whilst others would seem to struggle. In many cases, drawing is abandoned at childhood until later in life when embarking upon a leisure course. In such cases, strategic drawing exercises are necessary to help prevent a negative learning experience.

Two Modes of Seeing

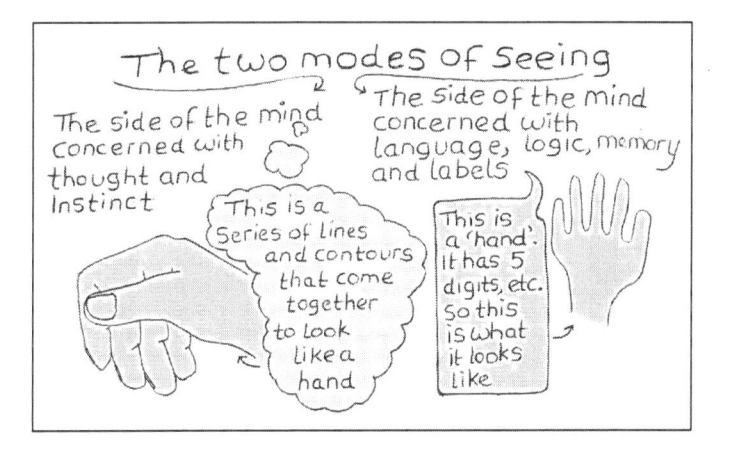

Students wishing to develop their drawing ability may explore how the brain perceives objects in two ways, as shown on the diagram, which might serve as a handout.

As can be seen, (in the most part) the brain's left hemisphere views things in their parts, it is logical, analytical, assigns labels to things and endeavours to make sense of the world. The right hemisphere sees holistically, is illogical and sees things as they really are.

Overcoming Picture Dyslexia

When presented with a chair, the left brain tells itself, "This is a chair." The chair has a square-shaped seat and four legs. All chairs have this in common.

The right brain simply sees the chair as a series of abstract shapes, and does not attempt to categorise it as having a square seat and four legs, or to tell itself, "This is a chair."

Abstract Shapes in Drawing

Students with low drawing ability may experience a dilemma between these two ways of seeing. A chair may have four legs, but all four might not be visible from a particular angle. The seat might be square, but the effect of foreshortening might make it appear squashed. The left brain sees only what it believes it sees; the right brain sees it as it really is. Betty Edwards' book, *Drawing on the Right Side of the Brain* (HarperCollins: 2001) explores this effect more fully and may be recommended to students concerned.

Step by Step Drawing Exercises

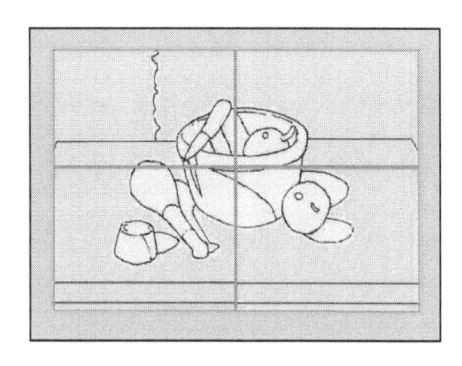

Learning to see entails forestalling the left side of the brain. The teacher may assist students with the following basic drawing exercises to aid drawing development.

Draw a narrow margin of equal thickness around the edges of the page where nothing may encroach, and a cross in the centre as shown. The aim is to plot the drawing from the central point and scale up so that the drawing inhabits a fair portion of each quadrant. This will guard against drawing too small or off-centre on the page.

Visually Plotting

Identify the central point of the drawing which will correspond with the central point of the page. Visually assess where lines and contours are in relation to the cross on the page. What aspects are positioned in the upper left quadrant, the lower right quadrant, and so forth?

Start with large elements and work down to the small. Identify a "key" measurement within the composition starting with the biggest. This could be the height of a pepper-pot or the width of an apple. This "key" may be used as a foundation from which to build up the sketch and make comparisons with other aspects of the composition. The pepper-pot, for instance may equal or half the width of a vase and so on. Find other key measurements and plot them onto the page.

A pencil or ruler may serve as a measuring tool. Close one eye and hold at arm's length to ensure consistency. Slide the thumb up or down the ruler until it matches the length concerned. Students are free to make visual estimates without any tools if they wish. The teacher may conduct a demonstration on this plotting technique to aid students.

Half close the eyes to break down the subject matter into a simplified jigsaw of outlines and tonal areas. Reflect this in the drawing, which will make visual judgments easier.

Kinaesthetic Drawing

Avoid sitting too close to the drawing for long periods, as this may cause inaccuracies to become invisible. Get up and stand at least ten feet from the drawing every fifteen minutes or so. This will force the brain to view the drawing holistically.

View the drawing in different ways. Turn the drawing upside down or view it through a mirror. Hold it up to the light so that lines will show through and in reverse. This will cause mistakes to become obvious.

Take a break for two minutes. Leave the room if necessary. This will reboot the brain and encourage a fresh viewpoint when the drawing is viewed again.

Flick the eyes at regular intervals from the scene to the drawing in order to get a comparison between the two.

Start light and work darker. The first line will never be accurate which is why drawing from light to dark is important. Mistakes can be overdrawn and accuracy built up as each adjustment is made. This prevents damaging the paper by constantly rubbing out or causing a messy drawing.

The objective of the lesson is to complete a simple line drawing by using the aforementioned strategies. Students may be encouraged to keep up or modify this drawing method for future studies.

Further exercises for developing drawing technique can be found in chapters 19 and 20: using a viewfinder as a drawing aid, and exploring negative space.

17. Taking a Line for a Walk Part 1: Random Mark-making

Objective 1: To make a random mark on a page by one continuous line.
Objective 2: To fill in at least two enclosed shapes with solid colour.

Some students may have difficulty putting pencil to paper or may need loosening-up exercises prior to the main art activity. Making random movements of a drawing instrument over the page is one such exercise. A progressive lesson on emulating Expressionism (in the next chapter) is optional.

Expressive Drawings

Taking a line for a walk involves randomly moving the pencil around the paper without it leaving the surface. The pencil, paper or both simultaneously (with help) can be moved around the worktop. Lines must occupy a good portion of all quadrants of the page.

The student may then fill in enclosed spaces with solid colour via oil paint or acrylic. An eye-catching design can be seen emerging as more white spaces are filled in, creating interesting lines and patterns.

Art Activity for Inclusive Learning

Taking a line for a walk is ideal for exploring line and colour without the need for prescriptive expectations such as drawing perspectives. It can easily be differentiated for different abilities, including those who need to develop hand to eye coordination or those who wish to create complex patterns.

Students may employ visual resources for inspiration or use a multitude of mark-making tools including different brushes, scratching implements or even fingers.

Inclusive Learning

Taking a line for a walk can be exercised whenever students feel the need. It can be a ten-minute loosening up exercise or form the foundation for a more ambitious project. It can be exercised by students of all abilities, assisting hand-to-eye coordination, provide opportunities for colour experimentation or complex art techniques.

18. *Taking a Line for a Walk Part 2: Emulating Expressionism*

Objective: To complete an abstract painting by using random marks and colours in an expressionist style.

Emulating the great Expressionist and Abstract artists may form a logical step forward for beginners in painting who wish to complete their first artwork but don't know how. The lesson might also form a natural progression from the previous lesson on taking a line for a walk. Abstract art is basically any non-representational artwork, in some cases, to express inner emotional states of the artist. Examples of such artists are:

- Wassily Kandinsky
- Oskar Kokoschka
- Joan Miro
- Jackson Pollock
- Paul Klee
- Robert Delaunay
- Kasimir Malevich
- Willem De Kooning
- Arshile Gorky
- Georgia O'Keefe
- Pablo Picasso

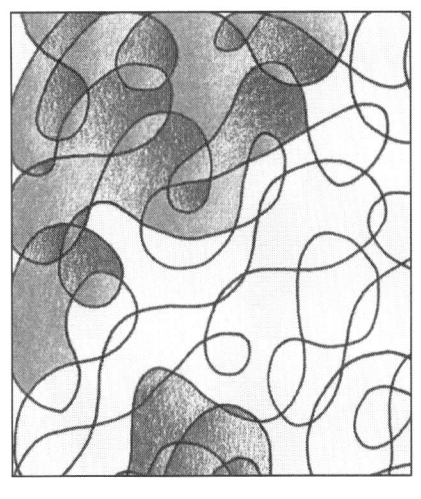

The work should not be an exact replica of the artwork selected, but one that emulates it. This means getting a general likeness with the way the paint has been applied and the style of the painting. Using solid, bright colours, basic shapes and expressive use of line, the beginner in painting may experience liberation from prescriptive objectives.

The German Expressionists

Imagery from Expressionist art can be used as a resource or to draw inspiration which, as students will discover was a purely subjective artform. Developed at the turn of the twentieth century, the two main schools of Expressionism were Der Blaue Reiter and Die Brucke which may be visually explored and incorporated into the artwork.

Students may render abstract shapes and lines around the painting surface or use everyday objects as a stencil such as seashells, combs, scissors, or randomly cutout shapes. Lines may be used to connect various elements together in order to create enclosed spaces and areas of background. Such an abstract composition may bring about a painting in the style of Miro or Kokoschka.

Elements of the painting can be filled in with either bright or subdued colours, according to the intended focal points. The painting may comprise of a variety of techniques, which may include stippling, scrubbing or crosshatching. Simply blocking in with bright colours may also bring about the desired effect.

Experimental Paintings

Students who are unsure of what to paint may benefit from a purely experimental exercise on colour behaviour, line and technique. Taking away prescriptive expectations enables students to complete a painting by using a free and expressive painting style.

An introductory lesson plan into abstract art can be found in chapter 67.

19. The Artist's Viewfinder

Objective 1: To make a viewfinder.
Objective 2: To sketch a composition using the viewfinder.

Students might be inspired by the many techniques and art mediums to choose from, but may feel stuck on where to begin. The art teacher may offer guidance by suggesting a tool known as the artist's viewfinder, which will help students find ideas for painting. This is a piece of card with a window cut into it, which can be used as a visual aid to find compositions for painting.

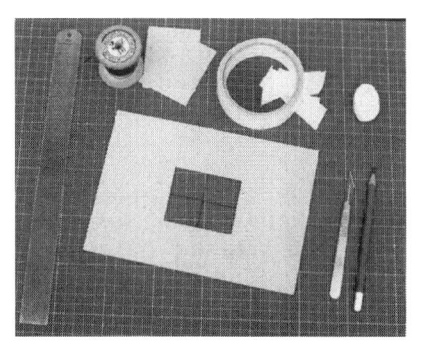

A Composition-finder

This lesson is split into two parts, which may be delivered as two separate lessons if desired. The first part is making the viewfinder; the second is how to use it.

The art teacher may begin the lesson by a demonstration on how to make a viewfinder. Alternatively, handouts can be supplied for students who prefer to read instructions. The following art materials are required:

- A cutting mat or old magazines to cut on
- A piece of card measuring 11 x 8 inches (20 x 28cm)
- Scissors
- Scalpel
- Pencil
- A steel ruler
- Double sided cellotape
- Cotton

65

Making the Viewfinder

The students may make their own viewfinder by simple steps:

1. Cut the card equally in half.
2. Draw a cross in the centre of each piece of card.
3. Carefully cut a rectangular hole in the centre of each card measuring 2.5 x 3 inches (6 x 7.5 cm).
4. Secure the cotton thread via the tape, to the centre point of an edge of the window and carefully stretch it across the window to the opposing edge. Place another piece of thread across the centre point of the top and bottom of the window. The thread should now form a cross over the window from central points.
5. The other piece of card can be fixed on top, sandwiching the edges of the cotton between the two.
6. Press the two pieces of card together to ensure they are securely stuck together. Trim any excess cotton from the edges.

The viewfinder in portrait mode.

The viewfinder in landscape mode.

Framing a Composition

The viewfinder acts like a frame from which compositions can be found. By closing one eye and peeking through the window, an edited version of the world can be seen. By moving the frame away from the eye, the view zooms in on an object; by moving the viewfinder towards the eye, a wider perspective of the world can be seen

Again, by holding the viewfinder in portrait mode, the top and bottom of the view will be emphasised; by holding the viewfinder in landscape mode, the width of the composition will be emphasised. The cross over the window will help students gauge the centre point of any view, and also work out how objects lie in relation to the cross. In this respect, the viewfinder is an ideal drawing aid for art class.

Students may make a simplified drawing of what can be seen through the aperture and transfer this image onto the drawing surface. Holding the viewfinder steadily will ensure consistency. Anything can be sketched at hand; a corner of the art room, a chair or part of a window. The aim is to simply sketch a series of lines as seen through the viewfinder.

Idea-finder

Students may put into practice what they have learned in the lesson to find a composition for a future painting. Using the viewfinder will help art students develop their observational skills which will in turn help develop their drawing abilities as mentioned. Furthermore, the viewfinder will reveal an interesting composition that may otherwise be overlooked with the naked eye. This is because the viewfinder edits out confusing clutter to enable students to make a clear decision on what may work as a painting.

Finding ideas on what to paint can be aided with the use of a viewfinder, which is a window cut into a piece of card. With its strategic use, the viewfinder can be used to find compositions from the most unlikely sources. Art students can use this art tool to compose still life, landscapes and figurative art.

20. Negative Space and Positive Shapes

Objective: To draw an outline of negative space around objects.

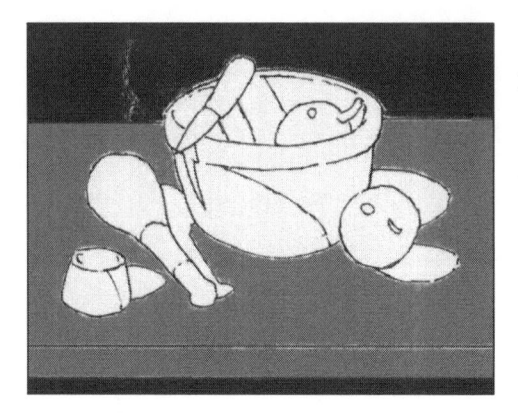

The composition for a painting will be enhanced if students are made aware of negative space that surrounds the main subject matter. Several objects of differing contours will be required for the lesson.

Background Shapes

Some students may not know what negative space is, in which case, a quiz, short presentation and/or discussion may pique interest. The teacher may then explain that negative space is the shape of the background around objects and give examples.

The teacher may then assign the students the task of observing the shape of the background between the objects students have chosen. This is known as negative space. Visual awareness of negative space will help students improve drawing skills and solve compositional problems. This can be achieved by the following methods:

Awareness of Negative Space

Encourage students to evaluate the distribution between negative space and positive shapes between their objects and to establish the following:

- Are there too many tall objects on one side of the setting creating a wedge shape to the background?

- Is there a big empty space in one area of the composition creating an imbalance?
- Are there repeating outlines within the composition, such as similar curves or straight lines?

Encourage students to shift their arrangements or shift the viewpoint to find solutions to compositional problems.

Painting Negative Space

Students may then colour the shape of the background as though it were the main subject matter. Using bright, contrasting colours onto paper will help students examine backgrounds in a new way. Differentiation can be supplied by using objects of varying outlines from the simple to the complex.

Enclosed negative space can be found between the slats of a chair or encircled within a cup handle. Students may similarly render these shapes in bright colours in order to exercise how such shapes relate to one another.

Background Features

Further exploration into negative space can be supplied by looking at the shapes of shadows, reflections or abrupt shifts in tone in backgrounds. Such features provide visual channels through which the eye may travel throughout the painting.

Chapter 68 explores the golden section, a magical proportion that fits into a visually-balanced painting. The golden section can be used to further enhance a painting composition or to solve other compositional problems.

21. Increments of Tones

Objective: To complete a light and shade study of objects in monochrome.

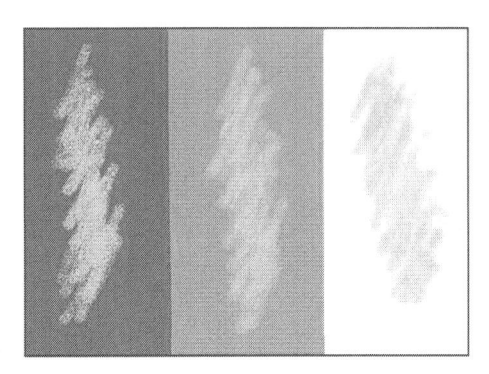

The tonal value of colours is often overlooked for its hue. A lesson heightening the awareness of tonal values of colours will help students make visual measurements of how one tone compares with another.

Colours in Context

The lesson may begin with a short demonstration on how colours appear in different contexts. The teacher may apply a pale colour onto a white background. Students may be asked to judge the colour's tonal value. The consensus is likely to be that the pale colour appears dark; on a dark background, it will appear overly pale. For this reason, painting onto a neutral-coloured background will reveal a colour's true tonal value. Pale blue, brown or grey acrylic under-paint will suffice. Students may then apply the oil paint on top of this neutral-coloured surface.

Exercise on Measuring Tones

The following painting exercise will further raise visual awareness of tones which can be utilised in painting.

Prior to the lesson, prepare objects of simple shapes, such as cuboids, spheroids and cylinders. These can easily be found in everyday objects such as matchboxes, cereal boxes, golf balls and biscuit tins. Paint them white. These can be arranged on a white sheet and placed near a good light source. This might be near a window or lamp.

Tonal Values in Art

The teacher may suggest strategies to help students enhance their tonal studies.

- Half close the eyes to visually simplify the arrangement.
- Divide into four basic areas: highlights, pales, mid-tones and darks.
- Block in the largest shapes first, using light brushstrokes.
- Begin with the mid-tones, working towards the lights, followed by the darks.
- View light and shade as abstract forms.
- Work into the detail lastly by applying highlights and adding definition to the darks.
- In some cases, shadows will vary in shade, some of which will be paler than others. Outlines too, will vary; some divisions being well-defined, others blurred.

Tone Measurer

A further aid can be used to help students record tonal values more accurately. Cut a strip of paper or card. Divide into equal squares and fill each square with a particular tonal value, beginning with the palest. This tonal strip can be placed in the background of the setting to assist students with comparing one tone with another. Chapter 34 explores the effect of light and dark further in reflected light.

A piece of card exhibiting tonal increments can be used to help students judge tones.

22. Using Photographs for Painting

Objective: To write a critical analysis of a photograph.

Photography forms a key element of the visual arts, as students often use them as a visual reference for painting. The ability to manipulate photographs is therefore important if students are able to utilise them at will.

Elements of a Photograph

Since the standard 35mm SLR (single lens reflex) has been superseded by digital photography, students need not have an intimate understanding of aperture settings, depth of field or shutter speeds to take good photographs, but high visual awareness is still necessary. This makes an elementary lesson on photography crucial.

The teacher may begin by showing students examples of good photographs and those containing unintentional elements. Understanding the differences between the two will help students gain control over what is on display in the viewfinder prior to pressing the release button. This can be achieved by discussing what went wrong (or right) with each photograph. Students may supply their own photographs and swap tips on taking good photographs.

Photograph Evaluation

The teacher may assign students the following task into photo evaluation. Each student is handed a photograph and must give an evaluation via the following points:

- What are the key elements of the photograph? (For example, sky, land, trees, other objects).
- How many elements are there in total?
- What is the intended focal point or subject matter?
- Describe the lighting conditions and the weather.
- Is any part of the photograph blurred?
- What lies at the edge of the image?
- Are there any bright colours?
- If you were asked to copy the photograph into a painting, which pigments would you use?
- Which painting techniques would you use?
- Make a projection of possible problems with painting any of the elements exhibited, such as intricate detail or subtle effects.

Simple Exercises in Photography

The session may conclude with an assessment of the results. The teacher may embark upon a problem-solving session, where students may propose ways of enhancing photography. The following might be suggested:

- Ensure the lens is free from unwanted objects, such as fingers or hair obscuring the view.
- Avoid taking shots into the light. This could cause a fogging out of the subject photographed. It is better to shoot back to the light (unless of course, the effect is intentional).
- Avoid using flash photography except as a fill-in, as this could make the subject matter appear flat. Detail would also be lost within the deep shadows.
- Similarly, avoid using artificial light, as this could create an unwanted colour cast, which may make the subject matter appear jaundiced. It is better to use natural daylight or a daylight bulb.
- Squeeze the release button gently to avoid camera shake if a tripod is not handy.

The teacher may conclude with a short presentation reinforcing what has been learned so far, and providing the following tips, which might be reinforced in handouts:

High Resolution Images

If high detail is required such as close-up photography of pets, ensure the light is good. A bright overcast day or sunlight means that a high resolution can be used. High resolution is any setting that is 100 ISO or below. The use of "portrait mode" on some camera's settings will often suffice. Avoid zooming in too closely as this may simply have the effect of cropping the image viewed through the lens. If the light is poor, a tripod is essential.

Background Elements

Watch out for background objects that may remain unnoticed until the photograph is taken. A lamppost emerging from behind an object or a bleached out sky could spoil an otherwise good image. The teacher may heighten students' visual awareness of background elements by encouraging them to use a viewfinder. (A lesson on making one can be found in chapter 19). Images that contain different backgrounds can also be used as a discussion point on why a particular background works better than another.

Inspiring Photographs

If inspired by a scene, students may take several photographs from different vantage points rather than just one. This will increase the likelihood of producing the ideal photograph to use within a design or painting. Often the most interesting photos are those taken from unusual angles or lighting. An object viewed from directly above might reveal unfamiliar contours or textures.

Photographic Modes

In the same way, students may be made aware of the two modes of photography, "landscape" and "portrait," as seen in chapter 19. The former will emphasise the width of the composition, such as a stretch of sea of land; the latter will emphasise the height of the composition, such as a hilltop or trees.

The Basics for Good Photography

Students on a painting course will benefit from a basic understanding of photography. This will save the inconvenience of having to retake snapshots if they do not work out. Issues such as a clear lens, good lighting and awareness of backgrounds will ensure optimum results when taking photographs for painting.

Guidance on photographing artwork for the final assessment can be found in chapter 71.

VI Lessons on Colour Use

23. Introduction to Colour Theory

Objective 1: To recite the primary and secondary colours.
Objective 2: To recite the definitions of colour terminology.
Objective 3: To mix colours as directed to establish the primary colours.

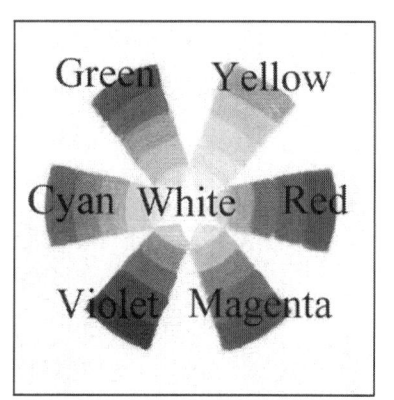

The colour theory forms a vital component of any scheme of work on painting. For this purpose, the art teacher may devise an introductory lesson plan on the meaning of colours and how colours mix.

What are the Primary Colours?

The art lesson may begin with a question and answer session to get the students engaged, starting with simple questions that may not necessarily be known by all. Indeed, what may seem obvious to some students may not be so obvious to others.

The questions may be thus:

- What are the primary colours?
- What is the definition of a primary colour?
- What are the secondary colours?
- What is the definition of a secondary colour?

The True Primary Colours

The teacher may assign students the task of researching into the meanings of these terms and to find imagery of colour wheels on the internet or from artbooks. The results are likely to be that colour wheels and other such charts will differ, as well as the colours featured. This is likely to spark a discussion.

The teacher may round off the session by giving the true definitions of colour terminology (given in a moment), which might be reinforced with handouts.

The lesson may progress onto an exploratory painting exercise on colour mixing by using oil pigments. The students may mix two apparent primary colours, for example, cadmium red with ultramarine. A surprise will be in store when a vibrant violet does not result, but a murky purple.

Students may be asked why this should happen. The answer will in fact be that impurities exist within natural pigments. Cadmium red contains a little yellow and ultramarine contains a little violet.

The Search for Primary Colours

It can be concluded therefore that not any red, yellow and blue are primary colours. The teacher may explain that the true primaries are those that resemble magenta, cyan and yellow of printing ink.

In terms of oil paint, manufacturers often use various colour labels for these hues. With visual resources exhibiting magenta, yellow and cyan, as well as paint colour charts, students may search for the closest match. Results might include permanent rose, process blue, pthalo blue or cadmium yellow (pale). The teacher may suggest that students include such pigments within their palettes for future painting.

In the meantime, students may mix other colour combinations (from red, yellow or blue) and then judge the purity of the resultant mix. Muddy colours will indicate that a lot of impurities exist within the pigments used.

A glossary of colour terminology will help reinforce what has been learned so far, as well as provide further basic information on colour theory.

Glossary of Colour Terminology

Primary Colour: A colour that cannot be mixed from two other colours. Red, yellow and blue may spring to mind, but not any red, yellow and blue is a primary colour. In fact, colours resembling magenta (not red), yellow and cyan of printing ink are true primary colours. In terms of oil paint, pthalo blue, permanent rose and cadmium yellow (pale) are close to the mark.

Secondary Colour: A colour that results from the mixture of any two primary colours. These are red, violet and green.

Tertiary Colour: A colour that is achieved by the mixture of a primary colour and a secondary colour. A tertiary colour will result for example by mixing yellow (a primary colour) with red (a secondary colour) to produce orange. Mixing cyan (a primary colour) with violet (a secondary colour) will produce violet-blue, and so forth.

Neutral Colours: An infinite array of greys, browns and neutrals can be achieved by mixing varying ratios of all three primary colours (and white, to adjust tone).

Harmonious Colours: Colours of a similar hue as can be found on neighbouring segments of the colour wheel. Orange and red are harmonious to one another, as are blue and violet.

Complementary colours: The opposite of harmonious colours, these are colours that lie on opposing segments of the colour wheel, such as green and red or violet and yellow. The two often clash and give high contrasts in painting.

24. Darkening Colours with Complimentaries

Objective: To paint a tonal-strip exhibiting a colour gradually darkened by the introduction of a complementary colour.

The causes of dirty colour mixes in oils are easy to tackle if students understand a little about how colours work and making a few adjustments in practice. The aim is therefore to darken a colour by mixing complimentaries.

Clean Colour Mixes

The teacher may begin with a short presentation on colour theory to consolidate the previous chapter and relate it to colour mixing.

The following questions may then be presented to students and suggestions put to discussion.

- Which pigments do you normally use to paint shadows?
- What colours would you use to darken foliage such as leaves?
- How would you tone down a garish colour, such as bright red?

The results are likely to be that some students use black to darken colours or use grey or brown to tone down bright colours. Some students might also express dissatisfaction with the result.

Mixing Complementary colours

The teacher may suggest an alternative method of achieving dark colours and neutrals, which is by mixing complementary colours. Complementary colours are those found on opposing segments of the colour wheel. Magenta is the complementary of green; violet of yellow, and so forth.

Colour-darkening Exercise

The following colour mixing exercise will help students achieve vibrant darks when rendering shadows or darkening a bright colour.

Select a bright colour. Green, red or yellow can be used.

- Apply this colour neat onto the painting surface.
- Add a little of this colour's complementary colour to the mix and place the mix next to the pure colour.
- Add a little more complementary colour and apply adjacent to the previous mix as before.
- Repeat the process until the colour mix is as dark as possible. Some might be black.
- The exercise may be repeated with another bright colour.

Students may self-evaluate the results and discuss problems with colour mixing. Perhaps too much of the complementary colour was added in the first instance, or the wrong type of brush was used.

Shadow Study

Students may practice this method of darkening colours by completing a simple still life study with shadows (see chapter 35). An apple, banana or strawberry would be ideal.

Students may discover that dark areas of shadow are rarely merely black, but often contain definite hues. Dark areas of a banana may contain mauve or violet. Students may add the complementary colour by certain degrees to achieve a particular dark. The darkest area may consist of an equal mix of the two complementary colours.

Avoiding Dirty Colours

Students may relate their experiences and exchange ideas on how the method can be improved upon.

The teacher may conclude the lesson by reinforcing what has been learned so far. The following suggestions will also help:

- Avoid adding black or grey to a colour to darken it.
- Avoid the inclusion of many earths, greys and neutrals in the palette.
- Never mix more than three colours to achieve a colour. This will deaden the mix.
- Try not to over-mix a colour. Leave a few streaks of colour on the brush to add a little life to the painting.
- Look for the opposing colour within darks of a particular object, such as green or greenish-blue within red tomatoes.

25. Mixing Greys and Neutral Colours

Objective: To mix at least four different types of grey in a painting from cool to warm, and pale to dark.

A colour mixing exercise in the form of painting grey and neutrals, as in a winter study, would provide an interesting oil painting lesson for art students.

Although rendering subject matter of bright colours, such as flowers and insects is a rewarding painting exercise, art students would benefit from producing an oil painting study of grey or neutral coloured objects. This would pose a challenge for students wishing to differentiate between different types of sombre colours.

The aim of this art lesson is to show students that contrary to first impressions, greys are not always a mixture of black and white, but a surprising array of colour mixtures. This will in turn develop observational skills in students when rendering water, shadows, clouds and wildlife.

Painting Grey

A painting lesson on neutral colours must include subject matter that interests the students. There is a wide choice available, including, moths, seashells, eggshells, stone, including stone circles (chapter 52), old boots, rusty tools, mist, water, relics, metal or storm clouds.

Prior to the painting task, the art teacher may conduct an introductory presentation and a question and answer session with students on how grey is mixed. Painting exemplars by artists such as Picasso, Pollock or Turner will dispel the notion that greys are simply a mixture of black and white. A prior art lesson on colour theory and colour behaviour (as covered in chapters 23 and 24) will further inform students on how to mix greys.

What is Grey?

Students may write descriptions or labels of all the greys and neutrals that can be seen. This may include: silver, eggshell, pewter, beige, steel, slate Paynes grey, Davys grey, neutral tint, buff, or even such descriptions as violet-grey, green-grey or blue-grey. Collating the results and transferring them onto a chart is likely to result in many descriptive words for grey, some of which may never be conceived by certain students.

Different Greys

With the above in mind, students may complete their "grey" study as suggested earlier by mixing at least four different greys. The use of black or ready-mixed grey pigment is prohibited. Students may take note of the following:

- What is the colour temperature of the grey? Is it warm or cool?
- Are there any colour shifts within the grey, such as can be found in clouds or mists?
- How does the grey appear against another grey? For example, mist may appear dark against a bright sky but pale against water.
- Is the grey translucent, opaque or somewhere between?
- Are outlines to different grey area harsh or blurred?

What Colours Make Grey?

Students will learn that various greys can be achieved with the mixture of bright colours, such as red and green, or violet and yellow with various amounts of white. This will alter the colour temperature and its tone. Earth colours may be used to soften the grey.

VII Lessons Exploring Painting techniques

26. Painting Dark to Light

Objective: To complete a painting from dark to light.

Painting from dark to light forces students to explore degrees of light and dark in a particular way. This is made possible by working on a black or dark art surface as opposed to a white one.

A Dark Art Surface

The usual practice of painting onto a pale art surface such as white stretched canvas or primed panel could mislead the art student on the true tonal value of a particular colour when applied on top. This problem is made worse if working under a bright light, where any colour, regardless of how pale, will appear much darker than it actually is. This could lead to an overly-pale painting.

Colours against Different Backgrounds

As seen in chapter 21, students may explore how the tonal values of colours may appear to differ when painted on different coloured backgrounds. Pale blue, for instance, will appear dark when placed on a white piece of paper, but will appear quite pale when placed on a black background.

Art students may supply the following art resources for the lesson:

- A black art surface. This might be an oil painting panel or stretched canvas, overlaid with black acrylic paint that has been allowed to dry.
- White pastel pencil or chalk for the drawing, which might be rendered beforehand.
- Pigments consisting of an array of tonal values, from pale to dark. Suggested pigments might be white, flesh tint, Naples yellow, sepia, burnt sienna, burnt umber, grey, indigo and dark grey. Bright colours can be used in selected parts of the painting to provide focal points. Alternatively, primary colours may be used with various increments of white.
- Subject matter or a photograph that features lots of lights and darks. This might be a still life study under oblique lighting, or a black and white photograph.

Technique for Shading

The teacher may perform a simple demonstration to inform the students on how to execute the painting. The following painting tips might help:

- Half-close the eyes and simplify the subject matter into four basic tonal areas: dark, mid-tones, pales and highlights.
- Begin with the darkest areas first which might be deep shadows or black objects. Use loose brush marks to block in shadows and subdued tones. This will force the students to differentiate between dark areas and mid-tones.
- Work progressively paler, blocking in the mid-tones next. Such areas might include reflected light and soft shadows.
- Keep working over the painting, using ever paler colours, which might represent soft areas of light and pale objects.
- Finish off with the highlights with neat white paint.

Tonal Outlines

Once the painting surface has been covered, students may examine how the outlines of tonal divisions differ; some shadows will have blurred edges, in which case, blending with a soft brush will be necessary. In other areas, tonal divisions will appear more defined, as in the case of highlights on glass or metal.

Exercise in Dark to Light

Painting from dark to light encourages the judgement of tonal degrees in a different way. The usual practice of painting onto a white surface could give a misleading impression of the true tonal value of the colours depicted. Painting onto a black art surface reverses this process and raises students' awareness of colours' tones. Simplifying the setting into four basic tonal areas will enable students to render a more accurate portrayal of tones in painting.

A lesson exploring increments of tones can be found in chapter 21.

27. Alla Prima Painting

Objective: To complete a painting in *alla prima*.

Painting in *alla prima* simply means completing a painting in one sitting and with one paint layer. A simple technique, and therefore ideal for beginners in oil, *alla prima* brings a freshness and immediacy to painting.

One Paint Layer

The art teacher may begin by showing students examples of *alla prima* oil paintings as completed by the French Impressionists, such as Monet and Pissarro. Students may take note of the painting style, such as loose brushstrokes and imperfect blends.

The art lesson may proceed to a demonstration on how to complete an oil painting in *alla prima*. A simple image may be used, consisting of two or three areas of colour. Generous amounts of pigment may be applied onto the palette, and ladled on briskly. Snap colour judgments are required and applied onto canvas within a limited time scale. The teacher may offer guidance as follows:

Art Materials for Alla Prima

For the painting exercise, students will require some or all of the following painting materials:

- A limited colour palette, including the primary colours and white. This will be titanium white, pthalo blue, cadmium yellow (pale), and permanent rose. A few earth colours can be included.
- Coarse bristle art brushes, such as hog or ox hair, no smaller than number 6.
- A cheap art board, which may consist of primed hardboard, card or even primed thick watercolour paper.
- Impasto medium to bulk the paint is optional, although paint can be scrubbed on thinly too.
- Palette knives and other mark making instruments may be used.

Basic Elements for Painting

Simple imagery will enable students to explore loose brushwork without fussy detail. Students may then discover how the brisk application of oil paint makes it possible to complete an expressive painting in one go.

Alla Prima Technique

The following oil painting tips will ensure effective *alla prima* paintings by the end of the lesson.

- Exclusive use of wide bristle brushes onto a relatively small painting surface will force the students to make economical marks on the painting.
- Avoid over-mixing colours, which will deaden the painting. Allow some colour streaks to remain.
- Using impasto medium will bulk up the paint, allowing students to explore mark-making instruments if need be, such as palette knives and old combs without having to use lots of oil paint.
- Half-closing the eyes will cut out irrelevant detail from the painting, forcing students to express only the most essential aspects of the visual resource, such as areas of light and dark.
- Standing back from the painting will enable students to see the painting on a smaller scale and record only what is vital.

Students should beware of getting bogged down with detail or of trying to perfect the painting. In such cases, completing the painting within a limited time scale may encourage briskness in painting style. This lesson may also be used to support the lesson on *plein air* painting, covered in section 10.

A Simple Art Technique

Alla prima is an oil painting practice which enables student to complete an oil painting in one go. The application of one paint layer via thick oil paint is the norm. Using simple art materials and a simple visual resource will make it possible for students to explore mark-making and brisk brushwork without regard for detail.

28. Painting Wet into Wet

Objective: To complete an experimental painting by using wet into wet.

Wet into wet is an art technique that entails working wet paint into wet paint. By applying runny colours onto a wet wash, or "glaze," interesting effects and happy accidents can be achieved, such as how colours bleed into one another. Using wet into wet techniques can be used to suggest reflections in water, skies, mists and soft tonal areas.

Oil Painting Washes

The art teacher may first show the students paintings featuring wet into wet techniques in oils, as can be seen in some of the early Dutch artists, such as Van Eyck. Students may then discuss how such effects were achieved.

Wet into Wet Demo

The art teacher may demonstrate wet into wet technique in front of the class and encourage volunteers to have a go. The following materials will be required:

- Size 6 or similar sable brushes.
- Small bottle of linseed oil.
- Primed paper or card.
- Red oil paint.

- Blue oil paint.
- Oil painting palette.
- Rags.
- Artists' white spirits.

Blue oil paint is diluted with linseed oil and applied onto the painting surface in a thin wash. Students may explore how colours bleed in chaotic ways by:

- Dropping a diluted red colour onto the wet surface and watch how it bleeds out.
- Applying the colour onto the wet surface with a brush.
- Try tilting the painting surface in different ways to see how the paint runs into one another.
- To experiment wet into wet with other colour combinations.

Students may critically evaluate the results and find solutions to problems. For instance, the colour mix might not have been sufficiently runny to apply as a wash.

More able students may explore painting wet into wet by experimenting with three colours or more. A further progression into completing a wet into wet painting may be provided for students wishing to achieve smudged effects of water or skies.

Using Wet Glazes

Applying wet glazes onto a wet paint layer is known as wet into wet. Experimenting with wet glazes is an ideal exercise for art students wishing to bring happy accidents into their paintings, to achieve smudged effects or to add mood.

29. Impasto Oil Painting

Objective: To complete a painting in impasto.

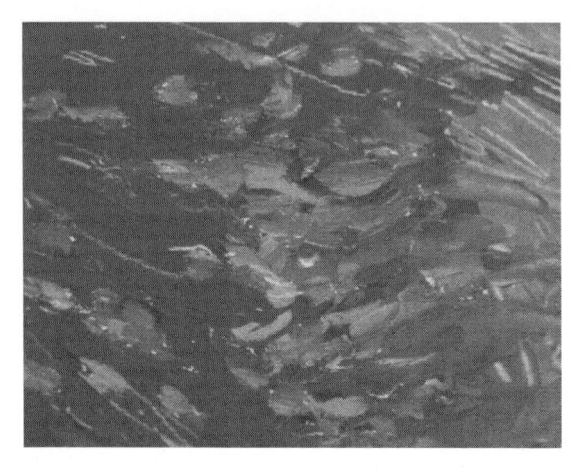

Impasto simply means the application of thick paint, creating interesting textures and the injection of expression.

Thick Paint Application

Pasting on the paint via a palette knife (explored in detail in chapter 31) or a stiff brush will leave discernable peaks and troughs in the paint. An impasto painting viewed under an oblique light will show up the textures, giving the painting an extra dimension. Van Gough's paintings are excellent examples of how impasto can add energy and movement, particularly to large areas of a painting.

Oil Painting Technique

A certain amount of boldness is required when painting impasto, but students may find the ladling on of thick oil paint a satisfying experience and may soon experiment with using other implements such as toothbrushes, spatulas and combs from which to create interesting marks.

Impasto Medium

Impasto medium (sometimes called oleopasto), an alkyd-based gel, is a useful addition to impasto application. This medium takes away the requirement of using lots of oil paint for producing textures to a painting, for it has the effect of adding body to the pigment. Students may alternatively add bulk to their pigments by using old or unwanted oil paints or even by adding sawdust. But for those using oleopasto, the teacher may offer the following guidance.

One's first encounter with impasto medium will surprise with its brownish colour. This need not be a cause for concern, for once it is mixed with the oil paint, the oleopasto will not affect its hue. The following serve as a guide:

- Gradually add the impasto medium to the paint in small amounts until the required consistency is reached.
- Try not to mix more than about half and half with the paint, otherwise the pigment will be spread too thinly within the medium and will lose its tinting strength.
- Once the impasto medium has been mixed with the pigment, the paint will stiffen and become bulky.
- Pick up a large dollop of the paint mixture and apply onto the painting surface thickly.

Applying Impasto

Students should watch out for applying the paint thinly or too evenly. Allowing peaks to remain will suggest textures to areas of the painting such as cornfields, skies or rustic elements. The paint can be applied in a diversity of thickness to achieve certain effects. Students may discover that areas of thick paint will appear to advance at the viewer and create focal points, whilst thinner layers of paint will appear to recede.

Activities exploring the use of palette knives and sgraffito technique (chapters 31 and 32) can be incorporated into this lesson if students wish to achieve other textures within the paint layer.

30. *Emulating the Impressionists*

Objective: To complete a painting in the style of the Impressionists.

Paintings in the manner of the French Impressionism at the turn of the 19th century enable students to employ loose brushwork and expressive colours. Reproductions of Impressionist art will support students wishing to emulate their style. Examples of notable Impressionist painters are:

- Claude Monet
- Pierre-Auguste Renoir
- Camille Pissarro
- George Seurat
- Edgar Degas
- Edouard Manet
- Paul Cezanne

Study into Impressionism

The French Impressionists were initially reviled for their brisk brushwork and suggestive lines which were not in keeping with the established oil painters of the time. Their exhibition at the Paris Salon in 1874 caused a revolution on how light and form can be expressed in art. The following qualities marked their Impressionist style painting:

- Loose wide impasto brushstrokes.
- Broken lines and imperfect glazes.
- Pure colours in certain places.
- Brisk completion of the painting, possibly in *alla prima*.
- Juxtaposition of opposing colours and tonal values.
- Suggestion of form as opposed to an illustrated approach.

Art Materials for Impressionism

The art students need to provide the following materials for the lesson.

- Wide bristle brushes no smaller than no 6. Flat or filbert sizes 6, and 12 (or thereabouts) and a round size 6 would be ideal.
- A limited colour palette, including the three primary colours, which in terms of oil pigments are cadmium yellow (pale), permanent rose and pthalo blue. French ultramarine, lemon yellow, burnt sienna and titanium white will also prove useful.
- Primed coarse linen canvas or textured paper.
- Artists' white spirits.

Photographic reference of landscape or figurative art featuring bright colours and contrasting tones applied with rich, buttery paint is best. Students are free to choose any Impressionist painting they wish but the following might spur ideas.

- Monet's paintings of London sunsets.
- Renoir's lily pads.
- Degas' ballet dancers.
- Manet's paintings of public interiors.
- Cezanne's still life studies.

Painting Techniques for Impressionism

The teacher may offer guidance whilst the work is in progress.

Stand back from the painting periodically. Sitting too close will give a misleading impression of the overall look of the artwork, as every small brushstroke will appear to have more significance than it really has.

Half-close the eyes to cut out irrelevant detail. This will help the art students express only the most important aspects of the painting and to practice economy with brushstrokes.

Resist the temptation to mix colours too evenly or to apply flat layers. Allow colour streaks and impasto marks to remain when applying the paint. This will help bring a sense of movement and vibrancy to the oil painting.

Do not attempt to emulate realism, as this is not what Impressionism is about. A painting that suggests form rather than detail will add expression to the painting.

Impressionist Colours

Bright colours were the mark of impressionism, which can be achieved by mixing opposing colours. Rather than use black to darken a colour, use it's complementary, as discussed in chapter 24. Consolidating what has been learned in chapter 23 on colour theory will also be necessary. Juxtaposing contrasting hues within a painting will create dazzling effects and chromatic focal points. This may entail placing bright colours next to subdued darks.

Impressionism in a Nutshell

Exploring how the impressionists used oil paint will help students learn about the properties of oil paint, regarding painting impasto and *alla prima*. Pushing colour contrast to the limits will also help students practice colour theory and how juxtaposing complementary colours can be used to create focal points and dazzling effects in an oil painting.

31. Using Palette Knives

Objective: To complete a painting by the use of palette knives.

Applying paint via a palette knife forms one of the main techniques for oils. The peaks and troughs that result will suggest texture, movement and energy.

Palette Knives

Palette knives are available in various shapes and sizes from those with a rounded tip to those with a sharp point. The type used for applying the paint onto the painting surface has a crooked handle to prevent paint getting onto the knuckles. Those that do not have a crooked handle are known as "mixing knives" and are used for mixing the paint on the palette.

Palette Knife Complimentaries

As described in chapter 29, an alky-based gel known as impasto medium can be used to add body to the paint, which can be used for creating textures when using palette knives. A full guide on how to use this gel can be found within the aforementioned chapter. Students may alternatively use unwanted or old oil paint to add bulk to the mixture.

An image featuring abrupt shifts in colour and tone will enable students to reflect these shifts in a textural way with the palette knife. A dramatic sunset, sea spray or sand dunes may spur ideas.

Palette Knife Exploration

Students may explore how paint behaves when applied with palette knives, by the following means:

- By the use of different widths of the palette knife, from wide to narrow.
- By applying the paint via different parts of the palette knife, using the blade flat-on, from the edge or at an angle.
- By ladling the paint via the palette knife onto a wet paint layer.
- By ladling the paint via the palette knife onto a dry surface.

Students may also explore how the paint behaves when applied in stipples, streaks or ridges. The crests and troughs that result will yield a relief effect, particularly when the painting is viewed under oblique lighting. Applying two contrasting colours via one stroke may yield smudged effects that might suggest a dramatic sky or ridges on mountains. Conversely, moving the palette knife in curves will yield a wavy result, which might suggest wavelets on a lake or river. A staggered or zigzag movement may suggest jagged rocks.

Techniques for Palette knives

Palette knives can be used in conjunction with impasto application (see chapter 29) to inject movement, energy and texture into a painting. Using various parts of the palette knife as well as different widths will create different marks. Similarly, moving the palette knife in different ways across the surface will create organic or smudged effects as desired.

32. Sgraffito Oil Painting

Objective: To complete a painting by the use of sgraffito.

Sgraffito involves scratching off an overlying paint layer in various patterns to reveal another paint layer beneath, adding movement and energy to the painting. Traditionally, sgraffito was used to decorate pottery and ceramics, but was also used by the Expressionists.

Introduction to Sgraffito

The art teacher may provide exemplars of sgraffito paintings, which can be found in such artists' work as Picasso or Matisse. A demonstration may also be conducted on the application of sgraffito by the use of old toothbrushes, combs, toothpicks, plastic cutlery, palette knives or the butt end of the brush.

Exploring Sgraffito

Impasto technique (chapter 29) may be used to enhance the effects of sgraffito for textural effects if desired. Impasto medium can be used to thicken the paint, although partially-dried oil paint can be used instead. Students must provide the following resources prior to the lesson:

- An array of scratching tools.
- An art surface prepared with a bright-coloured under-glaze, which must be a different colour to the predominant hues of the final painting.
- Impasto medium if applicable.

- Reference material such as an artistic influence, photographs or still life. The composition must be kept simple.

Scratching the Paint

Students may find out for themselves how mark-making can be used to achieve different effects. Using scratch marks to echo the outlines of the objects depicted, will add tension to the painting, as shown by Munch's the Scream. The French Fauves, such as Matisse's paintings shows how scratching off a paint layer to reveal a contrasting colour beneath can add shimmering effect to a painting. Students may also explore sgraffito to suggest textures. Sgraffito can be used in the following ways:

- By using different scratching tools.
- By scratching off a paint layer to reveal different colours beneath, whether it is darker, brighter or more subdued than the overlying colour.
- By using different scratching methods, which might be hatching, swirls or dots, to emulate splintered wood or creases in fabric.

Lesson on Sgraffito

Sgraffito is a simple painting technique that provides interesting effects. The only requirements are scratching tools, a paint thickener and contrasting colours depending upon the effect desired. Strategic use of sgraffito can be used to add texture, movement, tension or vibrancy to a painting. A lesson on using sgraffito to suggest animal fur can be found in chapter 62.

VIII Lessons on Still Life Painting

33. Composing a Still Life

Objective: To write an analysis of a still life composition.

Even the most accomplished oil painting techniques will not save a still life study if the objects within are badly composed. Students therefore need to know how to arrange a still life if an effective painting is to result.

Still Life Resources

The following items will be required for the art lesson:

- Samples of oil paintings depicting a still life.
- Examples of poorly composed still life paintings or photographs.
- Sets of three contrasting objects. A jug, a piece of cutlery and a plump fruit serve as suitable examples.
- A lamp.
- Pencils and paper.

The teacher may begin the lesson by showing examples of still life oil paintings that have been composed effectively and those, which appear out of balance.

Still Life Evaluation

Artist such as Chardin and Cezanne spent hours setting up their still life objects before painting them. In similar fashion, the students are assigned to make written observations on the following:

- How much background can be seen within the painting?
- What is the focal point of the painting?
- How many objects are there in the composition?
- Are there any contrasting colours in the painting?
- Are there any contrasting textures in the painting?

After evaluating the images, the students may engage in a practical exercise where the teacher provides three contrasting objects. The students may then arrange the objects to the best of their ability. Using a viewfinder (see chapter 19) will simplify the view, enabling students to see the composition in painting format. The following questions may spur a discussion:

1. How is the background affected by shifting the objects around? The background shape is known as "negative space." The objects themselves are the "positive shapes" (see chapter 20).
2. What happens if the light source is changed around? How does it affect the shape of the shadows, the tones of the objects and the overall mood of the setting?
3. How much "breathing space" does each object require? How is the composition affected by shifting the objects closer together or further apart?
4. What happens to the composition when viewed from different vantage points, such as from left to right or looking up or down upon the setting?
5. Look for echoes of contours. Is a similar contour found for example on the edge of a spoon and the edge of a jug?
6. What happens if the colours of the objects are shifted around? Examine colour juxtaposition.

7. Are there any reflections or residual light bouncing from one object to another? Such secondary light is known as "reflected light" and is explored in the next chapter. How does this affect the composition?

Still Life Balance

The students will discover for themselves the art of composing a still life study by trial and error. The following points may reinforce the lesson for the students.

- Evenly distributing the negative and positive space within a setting will bring balance within a composition.
- Awareness of where shadows fall will guard against shadows falling off the edge of the composition by accident.
- Awareness of breathing space around the objects will guard against a cramped-looking composition or that of too much space within one area.
- Examining the still life arrangement from different vantage points provides possibilities for more interesting or unusual compositions.
- Looking for repetitions in contours and using them strategically will create rhythm within the still life.
- Providing opportunities for reflections and reflected light may add dimension, mood or focal points to the painting.

Arranging Objects

Composing a still life study is an art in itself. By raising students' awareness in matters such as the negative space, the placement of the light-source, the placement of the objects, the vantage point and the shape of tonal/chromatic areas will form a firm foundation onto which to build a still life painting.

34. Reflected Light on a Spheroid

Objective: To paint a spherical object exhibiting reflected light.

Reflected light is a subtle phenomenon that occurs when light is reflected back into the shaded side of an object. A spherical object provides an ideal subject for exploring reflected light.

Subtle Observations

The teacher may first explain that objects rarely consist of merely a dark side and a light side. Reflected light can be seen within shadow. In its simplest form, it can be seen on spherical objects such as the moon. To see reflected light in its purest form, the object must mostly consist of one colour. An apple, lemon or golf ball would be suitable, although smooth objects would be ideal.

Steps for Completing a Reflected Light Study

Students may prepare a mid-toned art surface prior to the lesson. Applying a thin under-glaze of neutral or grey acrylic paint will kill the whiteness of the canvas, making it easier to judge tones (chapter 21 explores tones in context in full). The reflected light study can be completed in the following steps:

1. Place the spherical object onto a white surface such as a sheet of paper; this will magnify the effect of reflected light.
2. Visually divide the object into five areas of tone: highlight, light, mid-tone, dark and reflected light.

3. Half close the eyes and observe the arrangement of these five areas of tone. Start with the mid tones and work towards the highlight.
4. Repeat the process, working towards the shaded area, stopping short of the reflected light.
5. Pay special attention to the reflected light, observing colour and tonal shifts within.
6. Gently shade the background in order to bring out the highlight and the reflected light. Stand back to ensure the tones balance up.
7. Record the object's shadow that can be seen pooling over the paper in order to give the painting a sense of space.

Techniques for Shading

The teacher may offer the following tips to help students develop their painting technique: work the paint lightly in a similar direction, leaving highlighted areas and reflected light until last. Keep making visual comparisons, working gradually thicker. Blend out any jarring lines that may not be visible close-up. Stand back periodically from the painting to visually scale it down.

Students wishing to progress may explore the effects of reflected light on more complex objects such as ornaments. Other students may have a go at rendering reflected light using a limited palette or monochrome.

Reflected Light Exploration

Reflected light occurs when light is reflected back onto an object's dark side. Sensitive observation of reflected light will help students create three-dimensional effects via shading with paint. Reflected light can be rendered in monochrome or in full colour depending upon the student's ability and the effects required.

35. Shadows in Still Life

Objective 1: To write an evaluation of shadow formations in two still life paintings.
Objective 2: To paint a still life composition exhibiting shadows.

Composing still life objects for painting forms an essential element of any art course but can be a tricky task. Unforeseen problems caused by invisible elements become apparent only on the painting's completion.

Shadow Shapes

A vital part of negative space (see chapter 20) are the objects' shadows. Because shadows are not solid, they are often overlooked when setting up a still life. This could cause the painting composition to end up looking lopsided due to a shadow pooling off the edge of the page.

Shadow Observation

To begin with, students may examine two images of the same setting taken under different lighting conditions. Students will see that the same composition of objects could appear vastly different. Back-lit objects will appear dark; objects lit from the front will appear luminous and objects lit from the side will feature contrasts, textures and tonal gradations.

Students may make written observations of the following:

- Describe the shapes of the chief shadows in the paintings.
- Do the shadows echo the object which caused them? If not, what are the differences?
- What colours can be seen within the shadows?
- Do the tones vary within the shadows? Can reflected light be discerned? (See previous chapter).
- Do any of the shadows form a focal point or provide a visual channel to a focal point within the painting?

Students will discover the hue of the shadows will shift according to the light source. In some cases, blues, violets and greys will be observed, in others, crimsons, greens and browns. Objects such as potted plants or a glass tankard may cause bizarre or unexpected shadow shapes which could create a focal point.

Recording Shadows in Paint

With the above in mind, students may set up a still life composition, paying particular attention to the shadows. Two or three contrasting objects next to a good light source such as a window or lamp will provide opportunities for exploration.

Sensitively recording the shadows is the prime objective of the exercise, paying special attention to their shapes, the hues within and the tonal values. The painting need not be finished, but the shadows should be in their complete forms.

Using Shadows in Painting

Raised awareness of shadows within a still life will help students overcome compositional problems with painting and enhance the still life study. Such awareness of hues, textures and the shape of shadows will encourage students to sensitively observe shadows in painting, as opposed to reaching for black and expressing them as dark smudges.

36. Ellipses in Still Life

Objective: To paint an object with an ellipse.

Many household objects contain ellipses such as vases and bottles, but drawing ellipses form a common difficulty. However, a simple exercise will encourage students to include such objects within their still life studies.

Troubleshooting Ellipses

The teacher may begin by a short demonstration on drawing ellipses, including dos and don'ts. Things to be avoided are:

- Giving the ellipse sharp corners.
- Drawing the ellipse asymmetrically; the ellipse might slant to one side, or appear more open on one side than the other.
- Rendering the rim of the vessel as a single line without suggesting any depth to the rim depicted.
- Drawing dark lines around the ellipse, even though lines cannot always be seen on areas of the actual rim.
- Failing to accord the base of the cylindrical object with the rim at the top. A common mistake is drawing the base of the cylinder as a straight line, and the ellipse at the top as an ovoid.

Rules of Ellipses

Students are then assigned the task of drawing an ellipse on a chosen subject, which might be a cup, teapot, vase or other cylindrical forms. Handouts showing the following points might help during the drawing process.

1. Judge how "open" the ellipse is. Is it almost fully open, like an oval; is it akin to an eye shape?
2. At the apex of the cylinder, draw a faint cross. Use a ruler if necessary to ensure the cross is upright, level and centred.
3. Begin to sketch the ellipse faintly. Draw curved edges to the left and right of the cross (where the rim of the object will be) and a flattened curve at the upper and lower part of the cross.
4. Knit each element together using soft, curved lines.
5. Stand back to view the ellipse at a whole to ensure it is symmetrical. Turning the picture upside down will reveal deviances, unevenness or unwanted bends.
6. Adjust the curve of the ellipse representing the rim pointing towards the viewer so that it is slightly more curved than the rim pointing away.
7. Give the rim depth. Draw the inner and outer edges of the rim, giving the rim more width at the foreshortening points to the left and right of the ellipse. This under-drawing will serve as a guide when laying down highlights, shadows or detail on the vessel.
8. Observe the curve at the base of the cylindrical object or vessel. It will appear more pronounced than the ellipse at the top due to viewing the ellipse from above. Use the vertical line of the cross to plot the lowest part of the curve.

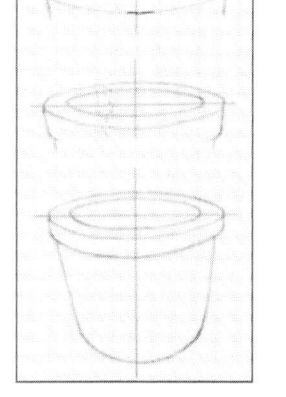

Drawing Elliptical Objects

Drawing ellipses is a common difficulty but simple drawing exercises involving a hypothetical cylinder will help students recognise faults and make changes. This means students may begin to view elliptical objects as an anticipated challenge rather than subject matter to avoid.

Students may then progress to more complex ellipses when ready, such as those exhibiting threads of a screw top or multi layered ellipses on decorative ornaments.

37. Objects in Foreshortening

Objective: To paint a long object in foreshortening.

Drawing an object in foreshortened view or in other words, pointing at the viewer, is a common stumbling block for students trying to paint from life. The "long" object often ends up looking squashed to one side, or out of true. The teacher may begin by explaining why drawing an object in foreshortening is a common problem.

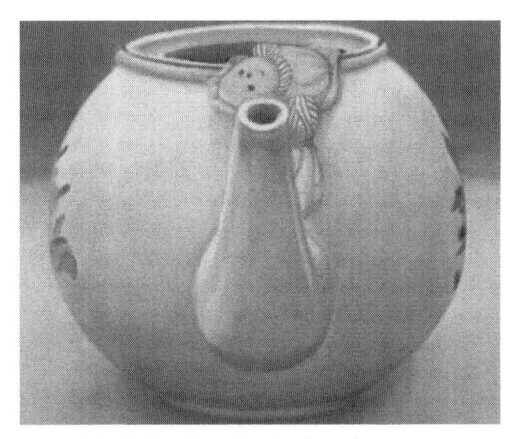

Troubleshooting Foreshortened Objects

Viewing an object in foreshortening causes a split view in the brain; the object is long and yet it appears short in real life. If taking on board both pieces of advice, the dilemma of how to illustrate the foreshortened object cannot be resolved. Exercises in the lessons on distorted perception in drawing (chapter 15) and how to improve on drawing ability (chapter 16) can be may be used as consolidation within this lesson.

The following drawing exercise might help with rendering foreshortened objects in still life art.

Tips for a Drawing Candidly

Long objects from the simple to the complex may be supplied by the students or the teacher, which might be clothes pegs, scissors, hairbrushes or bottles. Sketch two views: one as extended, the other in foreshortened view. Students may swap objects.

Drawing a pointing finger is a good alternative if no objects are to hand. Close one eye to eradicate the parallax view. Imagine the object is not three-dimensional but a flattened jigsaw of lines and tonal shapes. Retain this abstract view throughout the drawing process forgetting what the object is. Work lightly at first, working steadily darker. Follow the contours faithfully, regardless of how bizarre they might seem.

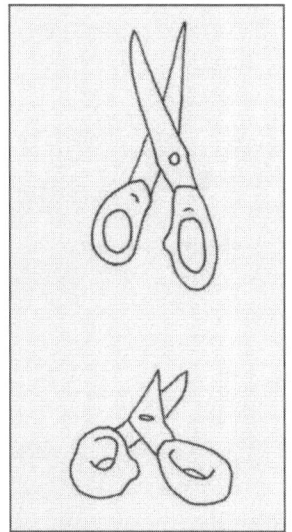

Overcoming Distorted Perceptions

Students are advised to forget labels for objects and forget any attempt at rendering what the object "is." Similarly, forget that it is long, curved or other descriptive labels for how the object "should" look.

The object is no longer an object but a series of abstract contours and tonal shapes that may often not exhibit lines, but areas of light and shadow. Resist the temptation to illustrate lines to demonstrate length if no lines can be seen.

More able students may have a go at more complex objects for a study in foreshortened view, such as candlesticks or binoculars.

38. Painting Reflections

Objective: To paint an object exhibiting reflections.

Shiny objects such as silverware, glass or china may bewilder some students who may not know how to tackle a multitude of reflections which may cause visual overload. Simple painting exercises will help students paint reflections on objects effectively.

Simplifying Reflections

Students should supply shiny objects without surface detail, which might be ornaments, bottles, glasses or silverware. A painting surface prepared with a mid-toned ground will also help students render highlights and reflections more accurately.

Complex lighting conditions as can be found in a multi-windowed room or fluorescent lighting should be avoided if possible. The teacher may instruct students to simplify the chosen object into basic areas of colour and tone.

Students should look for reflections that come in other forms as well as squares or pinpoints. Careful inspection may reveal an alien jigsaw of abstract shapes of varying hues and tones. White can in fact comprise only a small part of a reflection; violets, blues, greens and earth colours may also be seen. The outlines of reflections can vary from defined edges to no definable edges at all.

Technique for Painting Reflections

The teacher may assist students with the following guidelines when painting reflections.

1. With thin paint, sketch in the colour of the object possessing the reflection as though it has no reflection. This entails extending the hue of the object towards the reflection area. Do not add linseed oil or the paint's fluidness will make working on top difficult.
2. With slightly thicker paint, render the reflections on top.
3. Half close the eyes to simplify the shapes of the reflections into basic tonal areas. Make visual comparisons between the reflection and the surrounding area to ensure it keys in; is the reflection slightly paler, much paler, does it exhibit any hues?
4. Work from dark to pale, using increasingly thicker and paler paint, finishing off with bright highlights which might be rendered with neat white.
5. Retain objectivity by standing back from the painting. Ensure the shapes of the highlights are accurately depicted.
6. Avoid fussing over the area too much or it will lose its freshness.
7. Work over the area again, aiming for increased accuracy.

Smoothing Reflections

Look out for areas where the reflection merges with the local colour of the object such as those found on spheroids. Blending areas with a soft sable will ensure no tonal divisions remain. Working in smooth glazes (see chapter 63) also provides the ideal foundation onto which reflections can be painted. To achieve definition and an extra smooth finish, add a little linseed oil with the paint. This will help the paint flow.

The Colour of Highlights

Students are advised to observe the colour temperature of highlights, for many are not merely white. Some are warmer or cooler than others. Often the colour reflected will appear more subdued than the colour causing the reflection. The secret is to make comparisons between the reflection itself, the object onto which it appears and the surrounding area. This will ensure the reflection looks like it belongs to the object. More able students may tackle complex reflection shapes, as can be found on convoluted shiny objects such as animal ornaments or musical instruments.

39. Painting Flowers

Objective: To paint a plant exhibiting flowers.

Flowers often provide interesting shapes and colours for students to explore. Potted plants, herbs or sprays can be used in class. But flower heads such as poppies, roses, tulips or fuchsias could provide bold shapes and a diversity of colour and tones for experimentation and a variety of expression.

Resources for Floral Art

Producing paintings of flowers gives students the rare opportunity to use pure or outlandish colours. The resources should be high quality; photograph should be clear and the flowering plant should offer scope for several studies. Students may also experiment with taking flowers out of context to add interest to the painting. Floral art as completed by artists such as Georgia O'Keefe or Antoine Berjon will help provide inspiration for further exploration.

However, the plant selected should offer differentiation, in that some students may explore simple shapes, such as tulip heads, and others may have a go at the convoluted folds of roses.

Tips for Painting Flowers

Prior to the painting activity, the art teacher may offer the following guidance for students tackling the complexities of flower heads:

- Don't be afraid to use bright colours neat from the tube for expressing bold colours of flower heads.
- Applying the sunlit or pale colours before the shaded areas will ensure the pure colours of the flower heads will not be contaminated by a neighbouring dark colour.
- Don't use black to darken the colour of the petals, but its complementary colour, which is any opposing colour on the colour wheel (see chapter 23 and 24).
- Periodically standing back from the painting and using a wider brush than one might expect, will add boldness to any floral painting.
- A good quality sable is essential for detail. A number 3 or 6 round is often ideal.
- Over-mixing a colour might kill the life out of a bright colour. Allowing a few streaks to remain within a colour mix will add expression and life to any flower painting.
- Using exclusively bright colours could cause the flowers to look garish. Close inspection will reveal a host of subdued colours, darks and greys within flower heads.

Inspiration for Floral Art

The key to capturing flowering plants lies in working from the general to the particular. Half-close the eyes to simplify the plant into basic forms. Sensitive observation when working into detail is the key to capturing the truth of flowers. This includes looking for unexpected colours and bizarre contour shifts.

40. Painting Aged Objects

Objective: To produce a painting of an antiquated object.

Old or corroded objects in a still life such as rusty tools, antique ornaments or engine parts are sure to challenge students wishing to explore different textures to suggest wear and tear, peeling paint or rust. The teacher may offer guidance on the best art techniques to use for such effects.

Aged Effects in Paint

Students should provide examples of objects exhibiting oxidisation, peeling paint or other wear and tear. Some objects might offer interesting contrasts between blemished and unblemished areas, which can be suggested by using different techniques. Peeling paint can also add charm and visual textures to any still life. With several elements to consider, there is a choice of techniques students may employ, which can be

- *Alla prima* – the application of one paint layer in one session (see chapter 27).
- Sgraffito – the technique of scratching through the paint layer to reveal another beneath (see chapter 32).
- Or impasto oil painting – the application of thick paint (see chapter 29).

Good visual resources are vital for subtle effects such as rust. In this respect, little can compare to painting from life. An array of earth colours and neutrals will come in handy, as well as the essential primary colours. Burnt sienna, for example, can often be seen in oxidised metal; burnt umber in weathered iron.

The Colour of Rust

The teacher may offer the following guidance for students rendering old objects, beginning with rust:

1. Observe the rust's hue. Various amounts of burnt sienna, cadmium red, burnt umber, permanent rose and white occur most frequently in oxidised metal, although blues and violets may be seen in shaded areas.
2. Weathered iron often appears darker, in which case burnt umber, ultramarine and pthalo blue might be more in order. A thin under-glaze of burnt umber acrylic will support the overlying colours of either when applied.
3. Apply the paint briskly and unevenly for impasto effects via a filbert ox-hair. Allow a little of the under-glaze to show through in places. Sgraffito can be incorporated if suggesting a scratched surface or splintered wood.
4. Allow brush marks to remain. If peeling paint is featured on the object, apply the colour representing the paint thinly, working the paint roughly and unevenly.

Aged Wood

Sgraffito is a useful technique for suggesting splintered wood or similar textures. Scratching the paint layer via a sharp implement in the direction of the grain is great for suggesting wood grain.

The raised edges of cracked wood or paint can be brought out in sharp relief if casting crisp shadows. Good control of the paint is possible if a dark colour is applied neat rather than thinned, bringing an effect like crayon.

Do not apply the paint in linear fashion, but with uneven marks. The same technique can be used for highlights.

Flexibility in Painting Aged Objects

Students of various abilities may explore different ways of emulating aged textures, from simply scratching in one direction to moving the implement in more complex ways. Students may also experiment with various techniques to achieve a desired effect. Revisiting any of the previous lessons on art techniques may be used for consolidation.

IX Lessons on Landscape Art

41. The First Landscape Painting

Objective: To produce a landscape painting consisting of no more than four elements.

Producing a simple landscape painting will help students get to grips with understanding perspectives and recreating atmosphere with oil paint.

Landscape Painting Exercise

The students' first landscape painting should be derived from a simple landscape photograph which may depict basic elements which could be sky, mountains, water and a focal point such as a cluster of trees or a ruin. A receding object running from the foreground to the background will enable students to explore perspectives. This may be a river, a track or a drystone wall. A strong atmospheric element such as a passing rain shower, mist or a windswept sky will enable the students to inject expression and drama into a landscape scene.

Art Materials for Landscape Art

The following painting materials including the landscape photograph are required for the lesson:

- An art board or primed card no larger than 16"X 20" (40.6cm X 50.8cm).
- A coarse bristle brush.
- A no 3 round sable.
- A selection of oil colours as outlined in chapter 1 may be used, or simply the three primary colours and white.
- Small pot of artist's spirits.
- Rags.
- Painting palette.

A Simple Landscape

Once the drawing has been carefully transferred onto the painting surface, the teacher may instruct students to adhere to the following guidelines and to observe the following:

- Paint large areas before the detail.
- Mix no more than three colours within any colour mixture.
- Observe that the tones and colours of distant objects will appear slightly paler or muted compared to similarly-coloured objects closer by. The effect will be emphasised in misty weather.
- Idealising objects should be avoided. This often happens when painting from memory. Cotton wool clouds, lollipop trees and triangular mountains are common examples and can be avoided if copying faithfully from good visual resources.

Landscape Technique

Students should be encouraged to stand back and to view their paintings from a distance. Mistakes will become obvious when turning the painting upside down. Retain simplicity throughout: mix basic colours and use bold strokes. This will ensure students will complete the painting within the lesson.

42. Landscapes' Panoramas

Objective: To paint a landscape scene suggesting depth.

Creating a sense of distance is essential for painting dramatic scenery, such as Ayres Rock in Australia, the Grand Canyon in the United States, lavender fields in France or a British stone circle (chapter 52).

How to Suggest Distance

The teacher may provide visual resources depicting such landscapes, and students may take part in a brain-storming session where common factors within the images are observed, which might be:

- They are all split at some point by a horizon.
- The horizon is mostly unbroken.
- They all have big skies.
- They all have foregrounds that serve as a frame of reference to distance.
- All objects within the scene get smaller in relation to distance.
- Each scene has great depth.

Making a Landscape Scene Recede

Creating a sense of distance in panoramic views is quite simple, but the effect can easily be spoiled if not done incorrectly. The diagram shows that if the landscape and the sky were represented by a grid, they would recede with distance. The greatest distance is reached where the grid converges at the horizon. The more distant objects, including clouds and shadows, appear smaller and more regimented with distance.

Depth in Landscapes

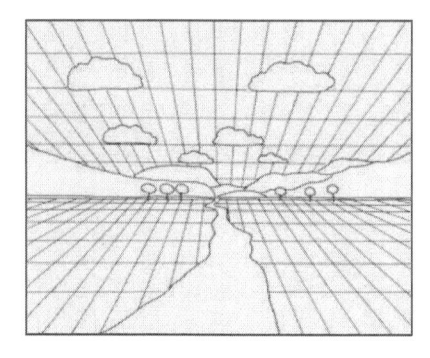

This sense of distance can be reinforced by the use of tones (see chapter 45) to suggest atmospheric conditions. Shifts of hue can be seen at various proximities. On a misty day, for instance, colours of distant objects such as trees and buildings will often appear increasingly paler, bluer or greyer. This can be seen to some degree even on a clear day.

A big sky can be emphasised if the horizon line were placed low down on the painting surface. This can emphasise a dramatic sunset or a looming storm. Placing the horizon line low on the canvas will have the effect of emphasising the ground, which might consist of canyons or a delta.

Creating Panorama

With the above in mind, students may embark upon their painting ensuring that:

- Consideration is given to the location of the horizon line.
- Objects of relative size appear smaller with distance.
- Objects of relative hue appear more muted with distance.
- The scene possesses foreground objects that offer a frame of reference to distant objects.

- A feature such as a drystone wall or river runs from the foreground to the background which adheres to the rules of perspective (more about perspectives in chapter 50).
- Sensitive observation of the scene will ensure it will convince the viewer.

43. Mixing Greens

Objective: To paint a green landscape exhibiting at least four different greens.

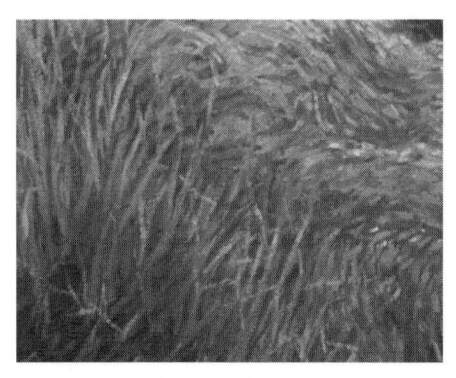

Few colours within the spectrum cause the problems that green does. Hence, when it comes to colour mixing, more has been written about this colour than any other. This is because green is found everywhere: trees, bushes, shrubs, forests and lawns. When trying to capture the vibrant colours of the landscape or the garden, the beginner will often be disappointed with the resultant blocks of green, green and more green on their painting.

Different Greens

Students should provide visual resources depicting green, whether this is a copse, forest, a grassy hillside or a garden setting.

The teacher may begin by raising students' awareness of the syndrome "green convenience," the view that green is simply a background for flowers of a gap-filler in the foreground. Consistently using the same green and yellow or a particular green throughout a painting will result in a flat and artificial representation of chlorophyll.

Blues and Yellows

The lesson may begin with a short exposition on colour theory, which might involve consolidating the lesson in chapter 23. The following points may be brought:

The cleanest, brightest yellow will be biased, even in the slightest way towards a neighbouring colour on the colour wheel, which might be green or orange. In the same way, blue will be biased towards violet or green. This is why any artist's palette should contain two blues and two yellows. Ones I would recommend are:

- Cadmium yellow (pale). This yellow has a warm glow, for it is slightly biased towards orange.
- Lemon yellow. This yellow is a fresher, acidic yellow, for it is slightly biased towards green.
- French Ultramarine. This blue is a warm transparent blue and is slightly biased towards violet.
- Pthalo blue. This blue is a sharp, cold and powerful blue and is slightly biased towards green.

The two blues and two yellows described will produce just about every green required, from autumn leaves to sunlit foliage in the garden. But, there is one green that has such powerful tinting strength, it would be useful within any artist's collection. This is viridian.

Viridian Green

Two schools of thought exist on viridian. This is because it is a very strong, artificial-looking green. When used alone, it will result in garish greens and amateurish-looking foliage. However, because it is such a powerful green, when mixed with another colour, it will result in beautiful greens. This colour is therefore recommended to students wishing to mix convincing greens.

Tempering Greens

A surprising amount of neutrals and earth colours exist within natural green. For this reason, burnt umber, burnt sienna or permanent rose are often required. Often the most surprising hues can be found in green.

Green Observation

The teacher may instruct the students to observe the scene as a jigsaw of different greens of at least four types. Each portion must be visually evaluated for colour mixing purposes, with the following questions:

1. What is the colour temperature of the green? Is it warm, requiring cadmium yellow or a little burnt sienna? Or is it cool, requiring more pthalo blue?
2. What is the colour bias of the green? Is it towards the yellow spectrum or the blue spectrum?
3. How dark or pale is the green? (Rather than use black to darken green, use its complementary colour, which is red – see chapter 24.) Permanent rose mixed with viridian, for instance, results in rich darks that can be seen in shaded foliage.
4. How muted is the green? Is it a pure, vivid green, or is it a greyish green? Does it exhibit any impurities such as reds or oranges?
5. How does a particular green relate to its neighbour in regards to colour temperature, hue and tone?

Students should trust their visual judgements and mix the colours as required to capture the green.

Authentic Greens

The aforementioned colours will produce almost any green found in nature from pine trees to iridescent chestnut leaves in autumn. Earth colours are often required to temper green, as well as green's complementary, red, to darken it. Sensitive observation will reveal that many greens exist in nature: violet-greens, crimson-greens and orange-greens.

44. Painting Snow

Objective: To paint a snow scene exhibiting shadows.

Painting a snowy landscape offers colour mixing challenges for students in that the subject matter is inherently white as opposed to a definite hue. However the art teacher may use strategies to help art students paint convincing snow, including how to darken it.

Snow Colours

Painting snow is a great painting exercise for practicing the colour theory, as unlikely colours as well as pales and neutrals can be found in snow, including blues, crimsons, violets and yellows. Darkening the colour of snow can also be achieved by mixing two complementary colours as opposed to using black. Consolidation on the lessons on colour theory (see chapters 23 and 24) might be necessary.

Pigments for Mixing Snow

The following important items are required:

- Good photographic resources, which may feature snow-capped mountains, a snowbound village or an icy lake.
- Artist pigments including the primary colours, cadmium yellow (pale), permanent rose and pthalo blue.
- The following pigments may also prove invaluable: titanium white, permanent rose, cadmium red, ultramarine, pthalo blue

and burnt sienna. Students may add others, but beware of mixing too many colours or the snow colours will end up looking dirty.
- Additional art mediums for enhancing snow effects. This might be impasto medium for thickening the paint or linseed oil for smooth glazes.

Tonal Key of Snow

Students may experience difficulty in judging the tonal values of a pale object when placed on a white painting surface. To counter this, the teacher may suggest a preparation of the painting surface with a neutral glaze of either brown or grey acrylic paint prior to the lesson. This midtone provides a useful benchmark from which to key in the lights and darks of the snow colours.

Darks and Pales within Snow

Some students may feel tempted to darken snow colours with black or dark grey, but this may result in heavy darks that lack depth. Instead, students are encouraged to look for hues in shadows. Blue for instance can often be seen in show on clear days. Such shadows can be darkened further by the addition of blue's complementary colour, red, or permanent rose. Similarly, the highlights in snow are often not merely white, but can be pink, cream, beige or eggshell. Looking for colours in dark and pale tones is a good exercise for raising awareness of colours in white objects.

Snow Textures

Students have the option to explore complementary techniques such as palette knives or impasto medium for thick layers of snow. Other students may have a go at simple blending techniques to make snow appear three-dimensional. This might involve grading a cream colour mix into a pale blue mix to illustrate a snow drift. Blending the paint with soft sables or a cloth will achieve smooth effects.

An Effective Snow Study

Painting snow is often a difficult subject matter for beginners, as its local colour is white. However, keen observation of snow's colour and tonal values under different lighting, will reveal blues, creams and even crimsons.

The application of a neutral colour on the painting surface prior to painting will make tonal judgments easier, particularly the highlights of snow.

Avoid using black to darken the colour of snow, as this will simply make the snow appear dirty. Finally, snow is also the ideal subject matter for exploring oil painting techniques such as impasto and glazing.

Snow Differentiation

Students of varying abilities may select an image of snow to match the level of challenge, from a single footprint or a snow drift, to the quilt-like and convoluted formations that drape over the rooftops of villages.

45. Effects for Mist and Fog

Objective: To produce a painting depicting mist or fog.

If it weren't for the atmosphere, the hues in the landscape would not appear to mute with distance. A convincing portrayal of mist is therefore essential if the painting is to convey atmospheric conditions.

Effects of Mist

The teacher and/or the students may provide visual resources that show how mist affects the apparent hues of objects.

The teacher may explain how tonal gradation and recession of a landscape give the scene a sense of depth. In addition, the landscape contains many aspects: meadows, cornfields, rapeseed, lakes, mountains and forests. The added variable of the atmosphere means that student must make further considerations in the colour selection when portraying atmospheric water vapour.

The Colour of Mist

Mist, as everyone knows, consists of water and varying amounts of impurities. But how does one capture such an elusive colour? Well, mist is made visible by how the dust and/or water particles partially obscure the view. This may be caused by reflections, the scattering of light, and how thick the haze is. The colour of mist will vary from landscape to landscape and in sunlight and shade.

Observation of Mist

As can be seen in the illustration, if the landscape and the sky are of similar colour and under similar lighting conditions, they will become paler with distance. This effect is relative according to the colour and tone of each object; a dark object further away for instance, may still appear darker than a pale object at close vicinity.

Similarly, a patchwork of different colours will be affected by recession in its own separate way, whether it is a lake, cornfield or mountain.

Mist over Vibrant Colours

Even a vibrant colour, such as the yellow of rapeseed or red of brick buildings will appear muted by mist. The teacher may suggest the following colour mixtures into the palette of an object's local colour to give the impression of mist or fog:

- Permanent rose, ultramarine and white.
- Burnt umber, pthalo blue and white.
- Pthalo blue and white.
- Or ultramarine and white.

Students may discover other colours, some unexpected which can be found within haze. Students are to make note of the following:

1. How pale or dark the mist is.
2. The presence of any definite hues within the mist (such as blue, crimson or violet).
3. The degree to which the mist obscures the view.
4. The manner in which it obscures the view. Some mist is patchy or pools into valleys, for instance.

Techniques for Mist Painting

Students may explore different ways of portraying mist or fog, but the teacher may offer suggestions where necessary. Smudging the paint thinly via a rag over selected areas will help imply ethereal edges. Dabbing paint with a soft wide brush such as a fan brush might be sufficient to yield soft effects. Dabbing the paint from the pad of a soft cloth is good for preserving detail adjacent to the mist area.

Exploration into Mist

Students may examine how other artists such as Constable or Monet achieved misty effects in sunsets or low cloud which may provide further inspiration. This will help raise students' visual awareness of the appearance of water droplets in the atmosphere and dispel stereotypical representations of mist within landscape painting.

46. Inclement Weather

Objective: To produce a painting depicting stormy weather.

Constable's later landscape paintings are well-known for their brooding quality. Indeed, there are many different approaches, methods and oil painting techniques that can be used to suggest atmospheric drama.

The Sky and Landscape

The teacher may explain that in order to produce a painting featuring inclement weather, the sky and the ground must not be treated as separate elements, as hues will be seen echoed in the other. A dark cloud mass for instance, will give everything a greenish tinge; a windswept sky will freshen the hues of the landscape.

Resources for a Stormy Painting

Visual resources will be required which might be the following:

- Photographs or a series of photographs featuring dramatic weather which might be a huge bank of cloud, lightning, gales or sheets of rain. The vantage point and the lighting conditions should be similar. This can be useful if a crucial detail such as lightning can be seen in one shot but not in the other.
- A series of sketches or drawings obtained from life.

- A palette of colours including the primary pigments, so that a colour can be darkened by introducing its complementary colour rather than black (see chapter 24).

Art Techniques for Inclement Weather

Students may use wide bristle brushes for impasto techniques on bulky cumulus clouds. But mist or drizzle can be achieved with soft sables and thinned oil paint or by smudging the paint with a cloth.

Scumbling is a good technique for suggesting broken clouds or a scudding sky. Scumbling is the application of a broken glaze by scrubbing thin but neat paint in a rough manner, revealing other colours beneath.

Sgraffito, where paint is scratched off, could be ideal for suggesting driving rain or hail. Toothpicks, combs, palette knives or brushes can be used.

Detail such as a ribbon of lightning and the fronds of windswept trees should be painted last and with slightly thicker paint.

Tips for Painting Weather

The teacher may assist students with rendering their chosen subject matter with the following tips:

Dispel presumptions such as "lightning is white," and "rain is grey." Any colour can be found within any such weather. Violet, for example can be found in rain; crimson in lightning and bright yellow in storm clouds.

Avoid using black when darkening colours in cloud masses for this could make the colour appear dirty. Instead use the complementary colour to the object darkened. Golden yellow as seen on cloud tops can be darkened with a little violet. Look for other colours in clouds, such as pinks, crimsons and umbers. More about painting clouds can be found in chapter 48

A Note about Painting Alfresco

Nothing quite compares to painting the elements from life. Teachers wishing to take students on a fieldtrip out of doors may do so with the guidance of section 10. The chapters therein covers the essentials such as the art materials required, including pochade boxes, preparing for the jaunt and dealing with people passing by. Students may wish to practice oil sketching the skyline or weather from a bedroom window or conservatory initially to practice painting under the pressure of a shifting element. Working in *alla prima* (chapter 27) is ideal for painting briskly.

47. Reflections in Water

Objective: To complete a painting featuring reflections in water.

The idea of painting water for the first time might be daunting for some students. The question often presents itself, "how do I make water look like water?"

The Rules of Water

Water as a subject matter is associated with complexity and confusion, and perceived to be suited only to the most competent artist. Some might even be put off the idea of painting water completely. This need not be so. The teacher may offer guidelines to help students overcoming the hurdle of painting water.

With the assistance of visual resources, students may use descriptive phrases to describe water under different weather conditions as in calm conditions, a slight breeze, windy weather and gales. The teacher may write these observations onto a whiteboard to find common features within each. The following suggestions may result.

A Calm Body of Water

In calm weather, reflections will resemble a mirror, and the upside-down image of the objects will appear directly below the objects themselves. Reflections of objects such as trees and houses will often appear to point straight downwards. The colours of the reflected object, such as skies and trees will often appear darker and more muted than the actual object.

Rippled Water

When the reflections of the water are rippled by a gentle breeze, disturbances will appear flattened by distance and stretch out in wide bands across the water. Where the sunlight catches the ripples, the dappled light will appear regimented within these bands. Closer to the viewer these disturbances will appear more random and diffuse. Vast stretches of water might still appear undisturbed despite a slight breeze disturbing other areas.

Choppy Waters

Where strong breezes affect the surface of the water, reflections of objects will appear broken up. The waves on the water will appear flattened by distance, but appear to contain diverse patterns closer to the viewer. Larger stretches of uniform colour will be observed on the water but lines of ripples will appear to move in uniform angles in one area.

Rough Waters

When the waters are subject to gales and gusts, the colour of the water will often appear grim, such as grey or slate blue or even white. The colour will appear uniform with little reflections to be seen. Crests might be seen breaking here and there, the more distant ones appearing in rows. Distant waters might appear to possess a slightly paler hue than the waters nearby.

Simplifying Water in Painting

With the observations in mind, students may use visual resources to paint water, but for the purposes of differentiation, images featuring water of varying complexities will enable all students to experience success in painting water. The teacher may offer guidance with the following tips:

Paint from the simple to the particular, breaking down the image into basic colours and tones. Details such as ripples and highlights can be added last.

Look out for unlikely colours in water, such as crimson and violets. Highlights are not necessarily just white, but can be cream or bluish white. Deep colours need not just be black, but dark brown or midnight blue.

Apply the mid-toned colours prior to the pales, but apply them thinly to avoid too much colour contamination of the pale colours. This will help set the tones of the water painting whilst it is in progress. Apply the darkest colours last.

Applying the paint thinly with a little linseed oil is ideal for creating smooth effects such as mist over the water or flat reflections. Impasto can be used for crests of foam.

Less able students may paint water exhibiting few elements, such as a flat stretch of water exhibiting one or two colours with few reflections. More able students may have a go at painting ripples and complex reflections.

Simplifying Water in Summary

Although water might seem to be a chaotic and complex subject matter, its appearance often adheres to certain rules when viewed in different weather conditions and lighting. Reflections for instance will always appear directly below the object and possess a slightly deeper hue. Ripples from a distance will appear as bands, where close by will appear less regimented. Close observation and practice will yield more secrets to painting this fascinating subject matter.

48. The Colour of Clouds

Objective: To render a painting dominated by sky.

The beginner in oil painting may fall into the trap of illustrating clouds as idealised cotton wool structures that dot a non-descript blue. But students will soon discover there is more to clouds than these candy-floss formations.

Types of Clouds

Visual resources and photographs will reveal the diversity of clouds on offer, but which are broken to down to basic types, which are: cirrus, cumulus, stratus and nimbus. Further cloud formations can be found in each type, such as altocumulus, or mackerel sky and cumulonimbus, or anvil cloud.

Resources for Painting Clouds

For the purposes of differentiation, various cloud images are required. Altocumulus is often more challenging to paint than cirrus, although each type of cloud will need a different approach. Students are required to prepare their painting surfaces with low horizons featuring a basic outline of the landscape. This brings the sky into focus and enables students to explore clouds in their own right. A lesson on painting stone circles in chapter 52 may set the ideal stage for a dramatic sky.

Palette of Clouds

The teacher may recommend the following pigments for skies, although other pigments might be used: titanium white, ultramarine, pthalo blue, permanent rose, ultramarine, burnt sienna and burnt umber. Round or filbert brushes (not brights, as they leave perpendicular marks) are ideal for impasto effects or for applying large areas of colour in skies. Good quality sable brushes are ideal for blending, but fine sables, sizes 3 and 6 are good for detail, such as defining the sharp edges of a thundercloud or the hooked ends of cirrus. Impasto medium will add bulk to the oil paint, suggesting texture to an impasto sky painting.

The Perspective of Clouds

Students may observe and/or discover the following during the painting process:

Clouds often follow the same rules of perspective as the ground. The bottoms of clouds often possess flat bases. The further the cloud formations are from the viewer, the more regimented they will appear to be. Formations at the zenith or directly above the viewer will appear more chaotic.

Outlines of Clouds

Look out for different types of outlines to the clouds. The tops of a tall cumulus cloud for instance will appear sharper and more defined than the formations closer to the ground. Students should take careful consideration to the most suitable painting technique to attain the desired

142

effect. Try out different applications within the same painting. If one technique fails to give the desired result, another can be tried. Sgraffito, scratches for example might be too harsh to express the subtle outlines of stratus, but smudging with a rag might yield the effect sought after.

Look out for different coloured pales as well as darks. Clouds are not merely white with grey shades. Creams, eggshell or china blue may be discerned as well as earth colours, violets or slates.

Tonal Contrasts in Clouds

Bizarre colours can often be seen reflecting off cumulus clouds during the oblique lighting of sunrise or sunset, such as dazzling reds, yellows and greens. Such subject matter might prove ideal for students wishing to explore colour behaviour or experimental techniques for skies.

On completing the painting, the teacher may suggest that the tonal values of the clouds key in to the rest of the painting, for instance, that the clouds are not too pale, making the sky appear bleached out, or too heavy, for that matter. Standing back from the painting and viewing it as a whole will enable students to key the sky into the landscape and to correct any tonal imbalances.

49. Sunset Hues

Objective: To complete a painting of a sunset.

Dawn and dusk are the ideal subject matter for students to build on confidence by exploring how colour and tone alter between zenith and horizon. Such variations are at their most pronounced during these times and can easily be portrayed.

Keying in the Sunset

The teacher may instruct students to bring a suitable photograph featuring a dramatic sunset, but also to prepare a painting surface with a thin wash of an earth colour to set the tones of the painting.

The teacher may offer guidance to students by encouraging the sensitive observation of colours of the sunset. Contrary to first impressions, sunsets do not exhibit exclusively bright colours, but also sombre darks. Without the darks, the bright colours would not appear so bright. Students may therefore take extra care to observe how these two elements relate to one another. Students are also advised to observe the shifts in hue between horizon to zenith and to take note of problems relating to colour mixing the transition. Dirty colour bands may result; the colour shift might also be too abrupt or patchy in places.

Elements of Sunsets

Lastly, students may pay attention to the silhouette of objects against the sky. The outlines are not always sharp and the colour is not always black.

Students may look for variations in the outlines as well as different types of darks.

Various painting techniques can be used to bring out certain visual effects. Sgrafitto for example can be used to suggest condensation trails in the upper atmosphere; "scumbling" a broken glaze to suggest scudding stratus clouds, or using palette knives for dense thunderheads in the distance. Suggesting texture to clouds by the use of these techniques can be highly effective.

An Effective Sunset Painting

Sunsets provide the ideal opportunity to explore stark contrasts in colour and tone, particularly in different cloud formations and skylines. Awareness of how bright colours juxtapose against sombre hues will contribute to a convincing portrayal of a sunset rather than one that appears artificial. Making strategic choices of the art techniques to achieve various effects such as textures or a broken glaze can be used to heighten the drama. Sunsets also provide the ideal opportunity to experiment with complementary colours (see chapter 24).

50. Perspectives of Buildings

Objective: To draw buildings by plotting and measuring as directed by the teacher.

The art teacher may help students learning to draw buildings get to grips with issues such as the vanishing point, measuring proportions and plotting angles.

Drawing Buildings from Scratch

Learning to sketch the perspective of buildings often poses challenges for students struggling with drawing, which is why a highly prescriptive art lesson is necessary to ensure success in the task.

How to Sketch Buildings

The art teacher may incorporate differentiation within the art lesson plan for less able students by simple drawing exercises of cuboids. More able students may tackle pictures of a cluster of buildings. This demonstration consists of a simplified line drawing of St. Mary's Church in Stratford upon Avon, England, offering various challenges for the students.

The art students require the following materials for the exercise:

- A simple image of a cluster of buildings (see diagram).
- Pencils.
- Erasers.
- Paper.
- Rulers.

Step by Step Exercise on Drawing Buildings

If the horizon cannot be seen, the students may sketch an imaginary line representing the horizon, remembering that the horizon is always at eye level.

The students must firstly find a common measurement within the image, starting with the biggest. In this case, the height of the church is roughly the same as the composition's width (top image). In this respect, the composition will be square.

This makes the centre of the composition easy to work out. The students can now locate the central point from which to plot the drawing.

Not everything will fit neatly. In this case the main tower is located just to the right of the image, so students may roughly sketch its location.

Now it is a matter of finding measurements in common from which to build the drawing, starting with the biggest. The width of the main tower equals half its height, for example. The annex extending from the tower to the left of the image is half as deep as its length, and so forth.

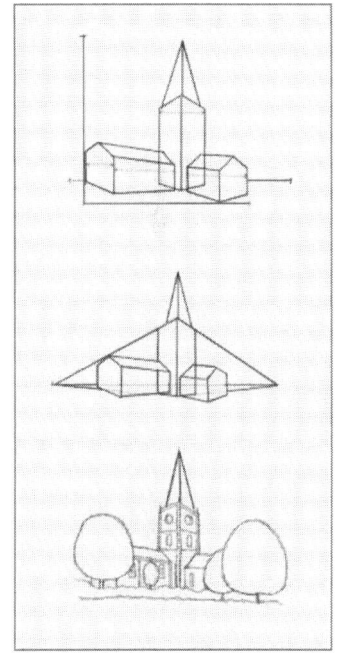

The students may continue to find common measurements within the drawing using rulers as measuring tools if necessary and by using the central mark as a point of reference.

The Vanishing Point

The vanishing point is a position on the horizon where converging angles from a structure such as a building or a road meets. The church having two visible sides exhibits two vanishing points on either side, (middle image.) Every building will generate its own vanishing point(s).

The location of the horizon line is important here, as it determines the steepness of the angles. The teacher may inform students that any aspect of the building that falls below the horizon line will generate angles that appear to recede upwards towards a vanishing point, as can be seen from the base of the church. A structure that lies above the horizon, such as the top of the church tower, will generate angles that appear to recede downwards towards the vanishing point.

Students may plot vanishing points by making visual estimates of the steepness of angles at the side of any building and where they converge when meeting on the horizon. Students will discover that receding surfaces will generate shallower angles when located near the horizon line; those located much higher or lower than the horizon line will generate steeper angles.

Detailed Drawings

With the basic plotting complete, the students may begin to sketch in detail (bottom image). Opportunities for individual expression can be used when sketching in windows, trees and bricks.

Plotting Buildings

Accurately estimating angles and the main proportions of perpendicular structures is what lies behind a successful drawing featuring perspectives; detail can then be easily filled in. Every student will be able to experience success with their drawings if the teacher allows for differentiation and is at hand to assist during difficulty, particularly with issues regarding the vanishing point and plotting.

It must be borne in mind that many buildings possess rustic contours and angles out of true, such as cottages and listed buildings, in which case, draftsman-like drawings will fail to capture the character of such buildings. This is why sensitive observation is always the key to effective drawing.

Lesson activities within chapters 15 and 16 on improving drawing technique may be referred to for students who experience particular difficulty.

51. Historical Village Scenes

Objective: To complete a painting featuring an historic village.

Plenty of quaint villages speckle Europe, including France, Germany, Italy and Britain to provide inspiration for an art class. This might be a treasured spot which holds childhood memories, or as a favoured holiday retreat. Furthermore, historic scenes of village offer a diversity of subject matter to tackle including buildings, figures and animals.

A Village Painting

A hiatus within an exacting art course can be provided in the form of producing rural paintings. The resultant artwork could be used as a gift, a greetings card design or simply as a focal point for the living room.

Most village scenes are ready-to-paint resources, having everything the student needs to produce a painting, such as focal points, which might be cottages, stone bridges, rivers, woods, churches, farms, buildings, animals and figures.

Period Villages

A village scene containing active elements which say something about the character of the village and the time period could add extra dimension and further challenges for students. Examples could be a field of hay bailers, a milking cart, children playing in the street or people going to church. Very old photographs of villages, such as those printed in sepia, might provide challenge for students wishing to explore monochrome or the use of a limited palette.

Figures in Photographs

A village scene containing figures and animals may put some students off, but the teacher may show that such elements need not be illustrated in full, but suggested with a mere brushstroke or two as did the industrial artist, L S Lowry. This may help get the reluctant art student get to grips with painting figures for the first time.

Artistic Editing

A particularly detailed photograph of a village could result in a painting that is too prescriptive. Students must think about what to include and what to omit when copying from such a photograph. Too much detail, such as lots of brickwork could rob the painting of focal points. Indeed, the composition could benefit from a little artistic license such as the shifting of elements or the cutting of an undesired object.

Buildings in Villages Scenes

The previous lesson on drawing buildings may be referred to if the scene contains a row of cottages or a church. A sound understanding of vanishing points and finding measurements in common will enable students to draw buildings accurately before laying down the paint.

Village Scenes in Painting

The ideal art lesson for students wishing to paint diverse subject matter in one go can be found in painting village scenes from photographs. The resultant artwork could be used as a gift or a greeting card design depending upon the time of year, or simply as a stepping stone to further artwork.

The painting exercise can be as easy or as challenging as the student wishes, for objects with different levels of difficulty can be found within. Added interest can be sought from old sepia photographs and active elements that say something about the character of the village and the times. The student must perform their own artistic editing and decide on the art technique and approach, although the teacher may make suggestions when asked to.

52. Stone Circles

Objective: To complete a painting featuring a stone circle.

Ancient stone circles such as Stonehenge in Wiltshire; Castlerigg in Cumbria or the Roll Right Stone Circle in Oxfordshire encourages artistic freedom without the concern for perspectives or vanishing points of buildings.

Such enigmatic locations also helps loosen up students who find it hard to express themselves freely, as the stones do not resemble an everyday object such as a chair or bottle. This means the student need not worry about whether it looks like that object or not.

Benefits of Stone Circles

An ancient stone circle is ideal for any artistic approach or expression, whether it is impressionist style or in high detail, meaning that any art technique, including *alla prima*, palette knives or oil washes can be used to great effect. But more specifically, an art lesson exploring stone circles will challenge students in the following ways:

- To explore neutral colours in the stone, moss or lichen, encouraging sensitive observation of subtle colour shifts.

(Chapters 21 and 25 can be referred to regarding mixing neutral colours).
- To explore how the weather has impacted upon the texture and hue of the stone.
- To explore how the weather can be used to add atmosphere and drama to the stone circle setting.
- To explore light and shadow, particularly in the texture of the stones themselves.
- To venture into abstract art. An ancient stone circle may instill various emotions within the artist which may be expressed in many different ways. An introductory lesson in abstract art can be found in chapter 67.
- To research into the stone circle. The information obtained could impact upon the completed artwork.

Observation of Stone Circles

There are many images of Stonehenge and Castlerigg to be found in magazines, the Net or students' own possession. The art teacher may encourage students to notice the difference between the stone circles. Some possess harsher outlines than others, and are set within different types of landscapes.

Stonehenge for instance, is set within a flat landscape and possesses straight lines and provides frames through which the distant landscape can be viewed. Castlerigg is set within mountains and possesses stones of a more organic shape. The Roll Right stone circle looks as though it is melting away. The students may select the most suitable art medium and artistic style to bring out a particular aspect of their chosen stone circle.

Suggested Colours for Stone

Students may explore the relationship between neutral colours and bright colours within the scene, and how both can be used to create visual channels throughout the painting. Many colours can be found within stone, but ultramarine, pthalo blue, burnt sienna, burnt umber, permanent rose and white may come in particularly useful.

Students may also make strategic decisions on the art technique to attain various effects, such as palette knives to suggest jagged textures or scumbling for lichen. The opportunity to explore the sky element as in chapter 48 or landscape's panorama, as in chapter 42 may provide the opportunity to consolidate what has been learned during these lessons.

X Lessons on Alfresco Oil Painting

53. Alfresco Painting Groundwork Part 1: What to Bring

Objective1: To recite a list of essential items for an alfresco painting fieldtrip (to be outlined in a previous lesson).
Objective 2: To prepare the aforementioned objects as discussed.
Objective 3: To make a homemade pochade box (if applicable).

An exciting art lesson, painting alfresco, or *en plein air* (in the open air), will present challenges for students, including observant spectators and painting under shifting light.

En Plein Air Painting

Taking an art class to a public place for painting *en plein air* requires extensive planning but the rewards could be immense, as students get to grips with painting as the French Impressionists did at the turn of the 19th century when practicing *alla prima* or impasto. But where should the teacher begin?

Ideal Locations for Alfresco Art

Inspirational public places for artists to paint are endless, from city suburbs to town squares. The following may spur ideas:

Historical villages and towns: namely Shakespeare's birthplace, Stratford upon Avon, Edinburgh, York or Bath. Or perhaps more grand places such as Tower Bridge in London, the Santorini villages in Greece, Provence in France, St Mark's Square in Venice, St Peter's Square in Rome or the Notre Dame Cathedral in Paris; but this may involve transporting art materials to a painting holiday. Public houses, gardens, castles or cathedrals may be found closer by.

However, an unassuming location such as a farm, park, gardens or street may offer equal inspiration and is more convenient. Bear in mind that what would seem to be an inspirational location for landscape painting may not measure up when producing the painting. The weather conditions for instance has a great impact upon the colours of the landscape and what may seem ideal during a sunny day or a dramatic sunset may appear featureless and empty on a dull day.

Essential Planning

The following issues must be addressed before planning an art fieldtrip to a public place:

- The distance to travel.
- Whether permission is required to set up a party of *plein air* painters in a particular location.
- Available places to sit or if mobile seats are required.
- Shelter if it rains.
- Special public events to avoid such as carnivals, processions or anniversaries.
- Special needs facilities including locality of public toilets or disabled access.
- Local geographical issues to avoid, such as wind-tunnels between buildings, busy spots where people continuously stream, noise levels or favoured pigeon roosts.
- The weather forecast.

The art teacher may conduct a trial run of the area to identify possible problems that may remain unforeseen until the day, or to discuss the event with an authorised local.

Essentials for Plein Air Painting

In order to make the day work, the art teacher may prep the students in advance on what to bring. Obviously weight is an issue. The art materials should be mobile and easily accessible which means omitting superfluous items and honing down to the essentials. It is advisable to bring only:

1. Primary colours, secondary colours and two earth colours. No more than ten tubes of oil paint are necessary.
2. Prefer short-handled brushes to long, as they are easier to store. Bring one type of art brush for each purpose, which might be a hog, sable, wide brush and a fine brush.
3. Transfer art mediums and solvents from large bottles to small plastic bottles with a tight screw top. Place the bottles in a plastic bag.
4. Bring disposable artist palettes as described in chapter 1.
5. Drawing implements for rendering a rudimentary sketch, such as pencils, pastels or chalk.
6. Plenty of clean rags and spare plastic bags for rubbish.
7. Bulldog clips to affix the painting onto a stable surface.
8. The viewfinder (chapter 19) may come in useful.

Other items to bring are:

9. Sun block, sunglasses and sunhat.
10. A thin waterproof raincoat
11. Insect spray.
12. A packed lunch plus a drink.
13. Spare tissues or wipes.
14. A foam rubber pad available from camping shops is compact and insulates the posterior against damp, cold or hard surfaces.

Students are free to bring other contraptions such as collapsible stools or sketching easels, but must take into account the added weight and bulk.

Students should pack everything in a large, sturdy, weatherproof rucksack. Separate compartments should be used for food and the art materials.

A Mobile Art Studio

The painting surface must be prepared before *plein air* painting. A surface no larger than A2 (420mm x 594 mm) in size is ideal. Primed board or canvas (not box canvases) would be suitable. A sturdy backing board and bulldog clips on which to affix the painting and the palette will provide a firm support and dispenses with the need for an easel. Alternatively, the art student may use a box easel or a homemade pochade box on which to affix the painting.

Transportation of Oil Paintings

Of course, minimal disturbance to the wet paintings during transit is essential, in which case, a pochade box with slotted compartments will come in handy. But not all are affordable. The following chapter describes how to make a homemade pochade box for protecting wet surfaces of oil paintings. The aforementioned chapter may be incorporated into this lesson where necessary, but students will need to be informed on what materials to bring.

54. Alfresco Painting Groundwork Part 2: The Homemade Pochade Box

Objective: To make a homemade pochade box for *plein air* painting.

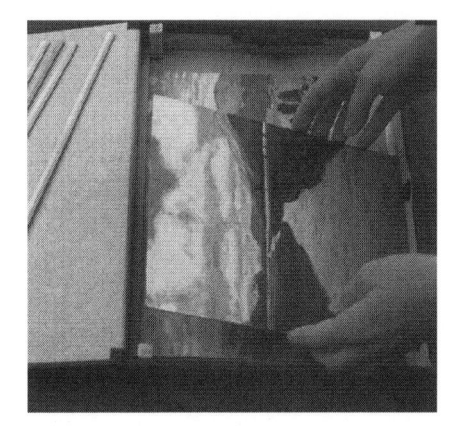

Oil painting in the open air is an exhilarating experience, but how do the students carry the wet paintings back over the countryside without ruining them? A practical contraption is required.

Painting out of doors is known as *plein air* painting. The Impressionists were well-known for this practice for they believed that the rendering of colours on location was the best way to capture the atmosphere. Indeed, nothing quite compares to sitting in a wood or on a mountain, absorbing the sights and smells and the shifting light. But difficulty is faced when carrying the wet paintings over terrain, risking paint-covered hands and a ruined painting. Before embarking upon the big step of painting from life, a little thought on how to transport the wet paintings is required.

The Artist's Pochade Box

Some specialist art shops stock travel kits designed for mobile artists as well as gadgets such as collapsible stools, lightweight easels and travel bags.

A contraption known as a "pochade box" is a hinged wooden box divided into compartments. The box opens up via a hinge like a laptop. The painting surface rests on the angled lid like an easel, where the painting is completed. The wet painting can then be slotted safely away without fear of the wet surface touching anything. These kits are not always widely available and can be costly. Making your own contraption might be a suitable alternative.

Materials Required

The image shows the materials needed for making a travel box for carrying wet paintings. These are:

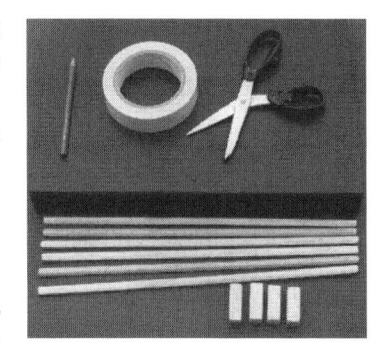

- A foolscap box file (usually manufactured in imperial sizes). This is a rectangular box with a hinged lid and sprung lever to hold the contents in place. Box files come in two sizes: A4 or foolscap. Foolscap is the one required. These are available in 10 x 14 inches (25.5 x 35.5cm) in area and needs to be 1.25 inches (3cm) deep.
- Six lengths of wooden beading, each 14 inches (35.5cm) in length (The same length as the box file). Beading is widely available in DIY stores and are easy to cut.
- Four 1.25 inch lengths (3cm) of rectangular balsa wood (or similar lightweight wood).
- Glue, or alternatively, double-sided sticky tape.
- Scissors.
- Pencil.

Assembling the Oil Painting Carrier

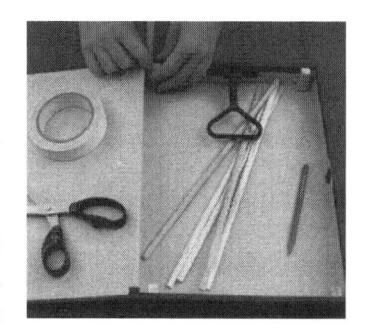

Place one end of the beading into a corner of the inside of the box. Allowing a gap of a millimetre or so, rest a block of balsa wood against the edge of the beading. Stick the balsa wood firmly onto the inner edge of the shorter sides of the box (not right into the corners) with double-sided tape. Repeat for the other three inner corners of the box as shown in the picture. The beading should slot easily into the gaps between the balsa wood and the inner corners of the box.

The box will allow the storage of oil paintings 10 x 14" (25.5cm x 35.5cm), 10 x 12" (30.5 x 25.5cm) and 10 x 8" (25.5 x 20cm) in size.

After completing a painting, slot a length of beading into each vertical side of the box via the gaps created by the balsa wood. Place the painting in the box face downwards. Only the edges of the painting will be in contact with the beading. If more than one painting has been completed, place more beading on top and place the second painting face downwards as before. Again, a negligible area of the wet painting surface will be in contact with anything. If a further painting has been completed, repeat as described, sandwiching more beading between each oil painting.

Always store the largest painting surface on top and ensure that it is facing downward. The other materials can then be stored inside the box without anything touching the wet painting.

A Wet Painting Carrier

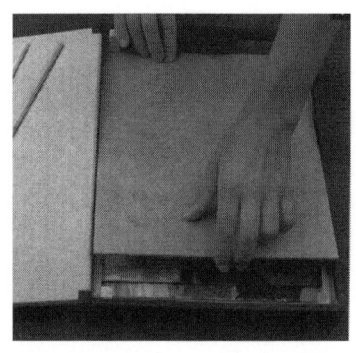

Painting on location is an exhilarating experience spoiled only by the risk of ruining the painting whilst carrying it back over fields. Pochade boxes are contraptions for the storage of the paintings and the art materials, but can be expensive and limited in availability. Making your own mobile studio is cheaper and offers more flexibility. It is quite easy to make and requires a few basic materials.

162

55. The First Plein Air Painting

Objective: To complete a painting *en plein air*.

Painting alfresco or painting *en plein air* as it is otherwise known, simply means painting outdoors from life. It is an exciting art activity for students who wish to have a go at something different and would like to escape the confines of the campus on a fine day.

An alfresco trip requires planning and the selection of a suitable painting site, preferably a quiet spot initially. These issues have been covered in the previous chapters.

The Shifting Light

Painting a still life outdoors will present the problem of the constantly shifting light. Students might be tempted to keep altering the shadows in accordance with reality, working over the painting until it loses its freshness. In other cases, the light might change before the painting is complete, the sun disappearing behind cloud or shifting behind a tree. For this reason, the teacher must encourage students to simply lay the brushmarks as quickly and as briskly as possible. A lesson on painting *alla prima* (chapter 27) is the ideal technique or *plein air* painting.

Before Painting

Students are encouraged to take a good look around for optimum views before setting down to painting. Using a viewfinder may help edit out the clutter and find the most suitable composition.

Comfort is paramount. Ensure the posterior is cushioned against hard surfaces. A folded coat or a foam pad found in camping shops will come in handy.

Watch out for sunlight bouncing off bright surfaces. Sunglasses or sitting in the shade will prevent the need to squint. Insect spray and/or extra layers of clothing might be needed when situation requires.

Tips for Painting Quickly

The teacher may offer the following advice for capturing the fleeting light:

Once everything is ready, don't procrastinate. Lay down the largest areas of the painting first. This might be portions of light and dark, a retaining wall or foliage in the background. Apply the paint thinly via a bristle, simplifying the view into basic areas. Detail and adjustments can then be made on top without the brush picking up unwanted surplus paint.

Use several brushes during the painting. This will save valuable time from repeatedly having to clean the brushes or mixing the same colours. Reserve brushes for darks, pales and other purposes.

Rather than work on one area at a time, render several areas of the painting simultaneously. This means picking up a "dark" brush, closely followed by a "pale" brush as the painting is worked over.

Record the most transient areas of light and dark first, making snap decisions on hue and tone. This means being decisive. Does that shadow contain blue or brown? Is that patch of sunlight crescent-shaped or triangular? Once the light has been rendered satisfactorily, don't be tempted to change them. Simply move on.

Add progressively thicker paint and work into the detail. This might be light skimming over a drystone wall or texture of crumbling walls. Don't worry if the setting no longer resembles the painting. Painting from life often means capturing the essence of a day rather than illustrating one moment in full as in the case of a photograph.

Completing the Painting

The final stages of the painting will often involve neatening and blending. This entails softening divisions between paint areas with a wide sable. Standing back from the painting at regular intervals will help students make honest comparisons with the setting. Absolute accuracy is not the objective, but the capturing of a particular mood or feel of the day.

Secrets to Plein Air Painting

Capturing the fleeting light entails using the paints in a decisive way and simplifying the view. Using several brushes at once will save time on cleaning them and remixing colours. Making strategic decisions on where the painting will take place will prevent un-preceded shadows from creeping across the setting before the painting is completed.

And lastly, allow robust brush-marks and colour streaks to remain. It is pointless to pursue perfection in a *plein air* landscape painting if time will not allow; the light will not wait. On completion, rubbish bags will come in useful for dirty palettes and rags.

Mentally preparing for possible spectators as in a public place is examined in the following chapter.

56. *Painting in a Public Place*

Objective: To complete a *plein air* painting in a public place.

Painting *en plein air* in a popular location such as a park, historical site or communal area provides its own set of challenges, not only from the constantly changing light, but from people viewing the paintings in progress. The teacher however may offer guidance on how to overcome these challenges.

Dealing with Viewers

Some artists enjoy having spectators whilst painting. Similarly, most people will admire street artists as they have the nerve to paint in a public place, often giving positive feedback. If the painting does not go to plan however, or if some students feel diffident, the art teacher may offer support in the following thoughts:

- Painting in a public place is often admired, regardless of how the painting turns out.
- Negative throw-away remarks can be cast off with the notion that the guilty party will never be encountered again nor possibly have the courage to paint in public.
- More often than not, spectators will forget the painting as soon as they pass on their travels.
- If any of the students are feeling particularly diffident at the prospect of painting in public, the teacher may set up their work stations in a quieter spot.

Ideal Public Locations

The challenges of the shifting light have been covered in the previous chapter. For this reason, students must consider the task at hand with the added factor of people walking by. Some students may wish to select a simple view, consisting of but four or five elements or part of the view. This may be a feature, aspect or sectioned view of the subject matter. Other students might be able to focus upon intricate detail without noticing what is going on around them.

Small Goals

But even the most complex subject matter may be simplified into four or five elements, which might be light hitting a window, statue or a skyline. Keeping it simple is the key to making the painting manageable, particularly if inquisitive viewers break concentration.

Setting small goals increases the prospect of all students coming away from the trip with at least a completed painting, whether or not it turns out as expected.

XI Lessons on Life Painting

57. Flesh Tones

Objective: To produce a painting of the human hand exhibiting flesh tones.

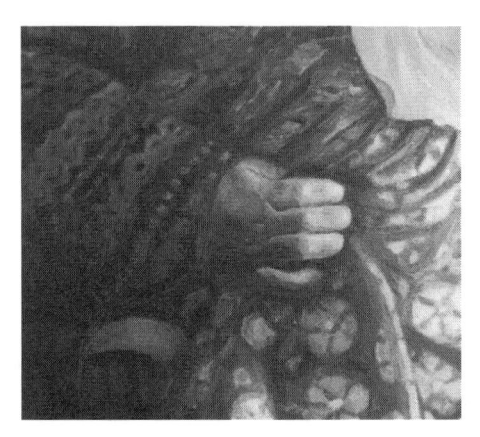

Capturing realistic skin tones in an oil painting can be difficult as the colour of flesh can easily look artificial. Preconceptions must be banished prior to embarking upon the painting exercise. This entails close examination of flesh tones.

Mixing Skin Colours

Students are assigned to explore flesh colours by rendering a painting of a hand – more accessible and simpler than other features such as a portrait. The painting may be worked from life (the student's own hand) or worked from a photograph. The resource must be clear, exhibit light and shade and have good clarity. The following pigments will also come in useful.

- Titanium white.
- Burnt sienna.
- Burnt umber.
- Cadmium red.
- Permanent rose.
- Ultramarine blue.
- Pthalo blue.

Shift in Hues

Tubes labelled "flesh tint" or "skin tone" should be avoided, for overuse of these colours will make the skin tone appear artificial.

Take the time to get the sketch right, but don't spend time rendering detail as the exercise is purely about flesh colours. Whilst painting the hand, students may observe the following:

- How one flesh area compares with another: is it cooler or warmer than the neighbouring colour? Burnt sienna is useful for adding warmth to the skin tone; ultramarine is good for cooling it down.
- Similarly, is it paler or darker?
- What is the shape of each chromatic area?
- What are the outlines of each chromatic area like? Is it smooth, gradual or defined?

The teacher may offer further guidance for mixing realistic skin colours:

- Convincing flesh colours can be achieved by just two or three oil colours.
- The slightest variation in colour and tone will have huge implications upon the appearance of the finished painting. Subtly is crucial.
- Half closing the eyes often helps to bring out and simplify the tonal areas of the hand and to give it form.
- Look for unexpected hues in the flesh colours, which might have a violet or greenish cast.

Tonal Key of Flesh Colours

As outlined in chapter 21, applying a pale colour, such as flesh tones, onto a pale painting surface will give a misleading impression of its tone. A thin under-glaze of mid-toned acrylic paint will help students judge more accurately the flesh colour's tone when applied in oils. Students must also be aware that whilst the painting is in progress, the hand will make little sense, particularly if the fingernails or creases have yet to be painted in. Once all the flesh colours have been blocked in, students may adjust the colours and the tones for further accuracy and a more faithful representation of the hues.

The Reality of Skin tones

Skin is not merely pink but often contains the most unexpected colours. Close observation is crucial if students are to portray realistic flesh tones accurately. Certain pigments will be more prevalent than others such as burnt sienna or cadmium red.

Don't use black to darken flesh tones or the colour will end up dirty. Instead, use an opposing colour. If the hue to be darkened is warm, add a little blue or burnt umber; if the area to be darkened has a cool cast, add a little permanent rose or burnt sienna.

Differentiation

Some students may wish to paint part of the hand, such as the thumb and adjoining finger, or the hand flat-on. More able students may have a go at painting the hand in sunlight and shadow or with textures.

58. Proportions of the Human Figure

Objective 1: To determine the average proportions of the human body in the art group.

Objective 2: To draw a simplified sketch of the human body in standing pose showing the correct proportions.

Learning how to draw the human body is an indispensable skill for art students if they wish to branch into fashion design or figure drawing.

But drawing the human form is often a trouble spot because of its complexity. However, the beginner may be assured that there is a formula to drawing the standing figure from which to develop life drawing.

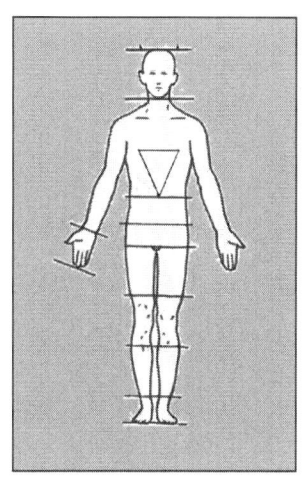

Exercise in Measuring the Body

The art lesson may begin with a preliminary exercise where the students may be divided into groups of four. One of the four will measure the height of each student's head and the full body height. The measurer must then establish how many heads make each student's body height. The results may be placed on a chart for comparison.

Students will discover that most will have a different height and different head length. The results however, are likely to show that most people will have different results but within a certain figure. Some people will have a body height equalling eight times their head length or slightly more; some seven or slightly less. The idealised fashion croquis features a figure nine or even ten head lengths high with overly long legs. The average human form however, is seven-and-a-half heads high.

Drawing the Idealised Human Form

The following guidelines will show how to draw the idealised human form which students may follow, although as demonstrated on the preliminary exercise, this will vary. The illustration shows the proportions of the idealised human form which may be used as a handout and a resource to support the drawing exercise.

- Draw a line to represent the form's central axis and total length.
- The top of the thighbone is located at half the body height.
- The length of the body equals seven-and-a-half head heights.
- The width of the head from ear to ear equals four-fifths of the head's length. The head may be expressed as an inverted egg shape.
- The length of the hand equals the width of the head from ear to ear.
- A perfect inverted triangle on the torso can be formed by intersecting the nipples with the belly button.
- The drawing may be completed by copying the contours of the figure, using the proportions as a key.

Common Errors

Due to distorted perception in drawing (see chapters 15 and 16) common mistakes may occur when drawing the human body. These are often:

- Drawing hands and feet too small.
- Drawing limbs too scrawny or short.
- Not drawing the skull deep enough.
- Drawing eyes too near the top of the head.

Life Drawing

Although nothing will compare to sensitive observation in drawing life models, the art students may practice drawing figures in standing pose by using the handouts provided which can be used to improve drawing ability. The formulas may serve as a useful guide when drawing or painting the standing human figure from life and may correct errors. However, as shown on the preliminary exercise on measuring the body, people slightly differ in their proportions.

Drawing in Symmetry

Students may also practice drawing in symmetry. Although the human form is not perfectly symmetrical, this is negligible when drawing the entire form. Drawing a symmetrical form can be done by working from a lightly-drawn central line. Viewing the image through a mirror or upside down will reveal deviations. A lesson plan on exploring symmetrical shapes can be found in chapter 65.

59. Painting Figures from a Photograph

Objective: To produce a figure painting from a photograph.

Tackling the challenging subject matter of painting figures for the first time can be daunting, which is why working from a photograph is best recommended.

A clear photograph is essential. (See chapter 22 on guidelines for taking clear snapshots.) Needless to say, good lighting, reasonable proximity and clarity are musts.

Preparation for a Figure Painting

Students are free to select the figure, whether it is a friend, relative or old photograph. A single figure will enable students to complete the painting by the end of the painting session. Prior to the lesson, students are advised to overlay their painting surfaces with a thin wash of neutral-coloured acrylic paint. This will make it easier to set the tones of the skin colours. Chapter 57 can be referred to regarding making visual comparisons between different areas of flesh.

Differentiation for Figure Painting

Some students may prefer to make a detailed sketch of the figure before coming to class. However, too much detail is unnecessary as the drawing will be overlaid with the paint. Care should also be taken that there is not too much background detail in the photograph which could take the focus from the figure. However, students are encouraged to edit out unnecessary elements when working on the painting.

Resources for Figure Painting

The following art materials are required for painting a figure from a photograph.

- Fine sable brushes, around 0, 3 or 6, for detail such as hair, eyes and highlights.
- The oil pigments: white, burnt sienna, burnt umber, ultramarine, permanent rose and cadmium red will come in most useful.
- As mentioned, suitable visual resources.
- Painting surface prepared as outlined earlier.
- Linseed oil to thin the paint to make it manageable.

Working from a Photograph

The teacher may offer the following tips for students painting figures for the first time:

Begin with the most exacting detail, such as the facial features and the hair whilst feeling most up to it. Work outwards towards simpler areas, such as the limbs, followed by the background.

Endeavour to cover the painting surface before the end of class. It will be necessary to revisit certain areas to balance out the painting, such as highlights and detail.

Make allowances for the painting looking "wrong" until features have been filled in, for example, eyebrows or the nose.

Flesh tones often contain deep darks and bright colours. Paint as candidly as possible. Standing back and viewing the painting through a mirror will reveal hidden mistakes.

Be forgiving. Figure painting is often seen as the last frontier of realism. If the first attempt does not work out, try again another time.

60. Painting the First Portrait

Objective 1: To draw the basic proportions of the head
Objective 2: To Embark upon a portrait painting (to be completed in two sessions).
Objective 3: To write an evaluation upon the portrait painting experience.

The idea of painting a portrait can seem very daunting. This is why a lesson on portraiture should consist of piecemeal achievable exercises. This will help instill success and encourage students to persist with more challenging exercises. To begin with, the teacher may inform students on the basic proportions of the face, which may serve as a guide. The following may be used as a template for the sketch.

1. Begin with an inverted egg shape which will serve as the basic face shape.
2. Lightly draw a vertical line in the centre which will serve as the axis.
3. Similarly, draw a horizontal central line. This is where the eyes are located.
4. Draw a horizontal line that falls midway between the central horizontal line and the chin. This will be where the bottom of the nose falls.
5. Again, draw a horizontal line just above the central point between the bottom of the nose and the chin. This is where the mouth will be located.
6. The ears fall roughly between the eye level and the bottom of the nose.

Of course, the above serves as a rough guide only. Nothing can compare to sensitive observation. Once the idealised sketch has been completed, the teacher may provide handouts for students to take home.

Resources for Portraiture

Portraiture can be an exacting process, which is why it might be necessary to allow two art lessons to complete the painting, unless, of course certain students decide to continue the painting at home. The following resources are vital for portraiture:

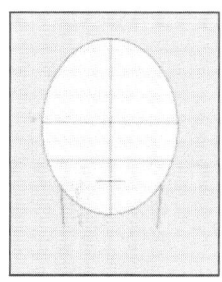

- A good clear photograph. Chapter 22 goes into detail on how to obtain the best photos for painting.
- Fine sable brushes for detail. Sizes 0, 1 or 3 would be ideal.
- The following pigments are often most prevalent in skin tones although others may be seen: white, burnt sienna, burnt umber, ultramarine, pthalo blue, permanent rose and cadmium red.
- An art board that has been prepared with a thin wash of neutral colour will help students judge tonal values more easily than if placing skin colours onto a white surface.
- Students may prepare the sketch prior to arriving at the lesson.

Reflection on Portraiture

Portraiture being an exacting subject matter requires lots of leeway and time allowance. The teacher may encourage students to reflect upon the portrait painting exercise afterwards in order to build upon confidence and improve. One such student of mine embarked upon a portrait, working from a good photograph. She managed to make sensitive recordings of the flesh tones and contours around the nose and mouth. However, on the second lesson, she had lost the photograph and worked on the eyes from memory, which resulted in idealised eyes. She was dissatisfied with the result. On reflection, she concluded that substituting memory for good visual resources had caused the problem.

Making Allowances

Students should be lenient when tackling a first portrait. The teacher may offer assistance with the following tips:

1. Thin the paint and apply the pale (not highlight) skin tones first.
2. Work progressively darker, taking care around the contours of the nose and around the eyes.
3. Accept that the portrait will look odd until certain elements have been filled in, such as the eyebrows and the eyes.
4. Don't rush areas like the eyes and the mouth. If tired, leave it until the next session when feeling most up to it.
5. Work darker still, filling in shadows beneath the chin or eyebrows.
6. Keep standing back from the painting to ensure the tones balance up. Make honest comparisons between the painting and the photograph regarding chromatic shapes and tonal values.
7. Work into the detail last, adding highlights and the darkest areas. Use thicker paint towards the end of the session.

On completion, reflect upon the exercise to establish ways of improvement or how the portrait could be done differently next time. The art technique, approach, the materials used and the visual resources may be evaluated in this way. The reflection should be around 200 to 500 words long.

61. Painting the Model from Life

Objective: To produce a figure painting from life as directed by the teacher.

Life drawing or painting can be an exciting experience. Having conducted life drawing classes myself, there are several factors to consider.

- The model. Required breaks, a changing room and a risk assessment (see guide on health and safety at the back of this book).
- Stools, chairs, couches and cushions will be necessary for comfort.
- The size of the room. Can it accommodate several standing easels, students and the life model?
- The lighting. Most life rooms have a north facing light, which enables students to study the form under relatively unchanging light. Otherwise, free standing lamps with coloured filters could be used.
- Props, such as clothing, backgrounds and furniture.
- Heating, particularly if the model is to be nude.

Painting from Life versus Photographs

Students will discover vital differences between painting from life and painting from photographs. Painting from life is not so "static," in that the scene presents more complexity; there is more background to be seen than on a photograph, the model as well as the student will shift, as will the light. Completion of the painting in one session is more important, as the life model is not as accessible as a photograph. However, during breaks, students are able to view other's interpretation of the same subject matter from different viewpoints and discuss their experiences. Assessments of the work may be conducted during the model's break.

Ideas for Life Painting Lessons

Students are advised not to get bogged down with detail or with getting one aspect of the life model exactly right. Work on the whole subject matter spontaneously rather than in parts. Stand back from the painting frequently and move around every now and then to reboot the brain. The teacher may devise a series of lessons on life painting, the following serving as suggestions, and which guidelines can be found in various chapters within this book.

1. Distorted perception in drawing (chapters 15 and 16).
2. Increments of tones (chapter 21).
3. Exploration of flesh colours (chapter 57).
4. Painting one aspect of the human form: hands, feet, the face or the torso.
5. Painting the life form in monochrome. This might be in black and white, a limited palette or in sepia.
6. Studying the form in terms of negative space and positive shapes (chapter 20).
7. Reflected light on the form (chapter 34). Coloured lights may be placed on both side of the model, such as red and blue.
8. Rendering the human form via different techniques: impasto, sgraffito, wet-into-wet, scumbling or palette knives (section vii).
9. Simplifying the form into essential chromatic shapes.
10. Painting dark to light (chapter 26).

There is endless scope for exploring the human form not mentioned here. The teacher is also able to easily differentiate the lesson plan to suit the ability of each student regarding one aspect of the form and the artistic approach.

62. Painting Wildlife in Sgraffito

Objective: To produce a painting of wildlife with sgraffito technique.

A popular subject matter, animal art provides opportunities for artistic expression and exploration. But in this case, using sgraffito to suggest plumage on birds or fur on mammals provides the ideal opportunity for students to experiment with oils to attain textured effects.

Textured Effects for Animal Art

Students are free to select the wildlife concerned for painting so long as it provides the ideal opportunity for etching technique. This might be feathers, fir, spikes, bristles, whiskers, tufts or a mane. From this, a wide array of subject matter can be selected from foxes and badgers to birds and otters.

A wide array of implements can be used for sgraffito. Sgraffito (explained fully in chapter 32) is a technique where an upper layer of paint is scratched off to reveal another beneath.

Emulating Animal Textures

Students are encouraged to explore different ways of applying sgraffito to attain a particular effect, which might be by the following means:

- The wideness of the scratching tool.
- The direction of movement.
- The spaces between each stroke.
- The manner in which the etching is applied, whether it is in swirls, crosshatches or in choppy lines.

Students will discover that a fine implement, such as s toothpick, might be ideal for emulating soft fur, particularly when stroked gently over the paint layer. Toothbrushes or combs might be ideal for suggesting plumage, exhibiting areas of parallel lines. The movement of the strokes, whether in choppy lines, crosshatched or in organic swirls might achieve effects for spikes, whiskers or a soft pelt.

Suggesting Anatomy

Students are also encouraged to take a look at colour shifts around the area of etching. For instance, how working from dark to light affects the appearance of an area of etching as opposed to using brash colours. Subtle shifts in hue can be effective for suggesting soft gradations in fur as on the flanks of a horse; abrupt tonal shifts can be used to suggest more convoluted areas, as can be seen on a dog's face.

Experimenting with *how* the colour is applied, whether by brush, sponge or a rag followed by etching may yield different results which can then be manipulated for effect.

Extent of Etching

Some students may wish to explore sgraffito further, completing a painting solely by using this technique. But others are free to use economy, which might be limited to areas of whiskers or the tail. Strategic use of sgraffito in this way can create focal points within the painting by shifts in visual texture, i.e., the difference between a smooth area and an etched area.

63. Glazing Technique for Animal Portraiture

Objective: To paint a portrait of an animal by glazing in three layers with oils (to be completed in 2 lessons.)

Animal portraiture is a popular subject matter for many reasons: to create a personalised dedication to a beloved pet, to produce a gift for a friend, a stepping stone into human portraiture, or simply for its own sake.

Challenges of Animal Portraiture

Like humans, animal faces differ as much as fingerprints. Dog faces, for example come in different shapes and sizes breed to breed and even within one breed. This is why it is important to banish generalisations and to beware of working to a formula. This lesson focuses upon achieving realism by using a technique known as glazing, where thin layers of oil paint are applied one on top of another in order to modify the colour beneath.

Alkyds

Students may venture into alkyd oil paints (chapter 1) which is like oil paint, but is thinner and dries quickly. Alternatively, to employ an art medium known as Liquin, which is an alkyd-based modifier that will accelerate the drying time of traditional oil paint.

Prior to the art class, the students may prepare their art boards with an underwash of a dark acrylic colour – dark brown, blue or black – which will work as the first glaze. A rough sketch rendered in chalk or pastel pencil should be completed on top. Of course, good photographic reference of the animal's face (see chapter 22 for guidance on photography) is also essential.

Glazing in Oils

It is not possible to complete a glazed oil painting in one lesson, as each layer must dry before the next layer is applied. Oils take around a week or so to become touch-dry, hence the need for two lessons. Liquin will accelerate this drying time, and should be used exactly like linseed oil, adding a little to the paint mixture as required. On the second glaze, students should work dark to light, applying thin glazes of oil colour over the dark underglaze. Students may explore the following effects:

- How thinner colour mixtures allow more of the underglaze to show through, i.e. when mixing the colour with a lot of Liquin, leaving an effect like stained glass.
- How a more opaque colour mixture obscures the underglaze, almost cancelling it out.
- Applying the paint with different utensils and brushes gives diverse results.
- How by adding a little of the medium increases control of the paint.
- How by shifting the ratio of Liquin with the paint in one glaze gives smooth gradations.

Students may continue to work from dark to light starting with large tonal area such as the planes of the cheekbones and the bridge of the snout. More opaque paint mixtures can be used for detail, such as the highlights of the eyes and nose. If an area does not work out, the next glazing session can be used to correct the problem or modify the colour further.

The Third Glaze

The paint should be dry by the following lesson but students are free to touch up their paintings at home. The following lesson progresses in the same way as this one, but students will discover how by adding this third glaze yields different results to the previous glaze in the following ways:

- Colours appear richer and deeper.
- Detail on top of detail sharpens the detail further.
- Colours can be modified further by adding this third glaze, whether it is to make it appear darker, paler or towards a particular colour shift.
- Applying one colour glaze on top of another yields different results to simply mixing the same two colours together.
- Applying subsequent glazes will smooth over blemishes and imperfections to create soft effects.

Completing the Portrait

Students may apply a fourth glaze at home once the paint is dry to touch up selected areas. Chapters 21 (increments of tones) and 26 (working dark to light in more detail) may be referred to in this lesson. Students should remember to make sensitive observations of the animal portrait throughout, such as folds of skin around the nose, fur around the ears and the tones of the muzzle. Turning the image and painting upside down will help students examine the image more honestly and to make accurate comparisons.

64. Organic Patterns in Nature

Objective: To produce a painting exhibiting patterns from nature.

The patterns that nature present are endless, from stripes on a tiger, spots on a leopard, speckles on an owl to markings on a seashell. Producing a painting of organic patterns enables students to practice hand coordination, examine how one colour sits against the other and how the shapes of each colour creates visual channels throughout the painting.

Creature Patterns

Students are free to select an image for study, so long as it exhibits patterns on a creature. The image can be part or whole of the creature, a close up or it can sourced from another artist. Rousseau, Picasso and O'Keefe are three artists who experimented with organic patterns in their art.

Exploration of Patterns

The teacher may make suggestions in how students produce their artwork:

- The colours used can be surreal; students may reverse or heighten the colours of the patterns – blue stripes or red spots for example.

- Textures can be used to amplify the patterns. Spots applied via impasto medium or etching techniques for stripes can be used to heighten contrast.
- The image can be reversed, distorted or altered in any other way.

Resources for Patterned Art

Cuttings and photographs of images featuring patterns in nature can be found in magazines as well as books. The image need not be crystal clear, but should provide adequate visual information on the nature of the pattern. Students are free to combine two or more images for their finished artwork.

Stepping Stone into Abstract Art

Any art technique and an array of mediums can be used for exploration, as outlined in section vii on painting techniques. Students may endeavour for a highly-detailed finish or a rough oil sketch, but it must show evidence of strategic planning, for example in the effect desired. This does not mean that the painting should go exactly as planned, but evolve as the exercise is completed. This might inspire students to produce further studies or venture into abstract art, explored in the next section.

Patterns for Design

Finding patterns in nature can prove useful for students wishing to venture into another area of the visual arts, such as dress design or interior design. The image can be as simple or as complex as the student wishes, or can be used as a repeat design or a motif.

XII Lesson for Further Exploration

65. Painting Symmetry

Objective 1: To explain different types of symmetry.
Objective 2: To produce a painting featuring at least one symmetrical shape.

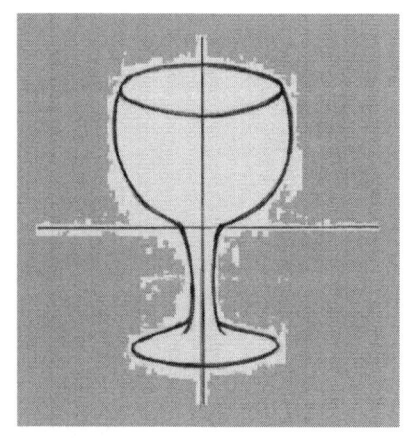

Exploring symmetrical shapes in the natural or synthetic world, like the previous chapter on patterns, may yield inspiration for students wishing to find designs for their artwork or ideas for further exploration.

Exploring Symmetry

The teacher may firstly explain that symmetry can be found in the natural world and in the manmade. In its simplest form, a symmetrical shape has two identical sides, one in reverse of the other. Most organic objects fall into this category, such as butterflies and beetles. Many geometric shapes are symmetrical too, such as triangles and squares.

Discussing Symmetry

A round robin session may ensue, where each student may give examples of where symmetrical shapes can be found. A summarising list could be given within an assignment brief, which may reflect the scheme of work.

Following the preliminary exercise, the teacher may reinforce what has been learned by explaining the different types of symmetry and terminology, which are as follows:

- A line of symmetry is a mirror or fold line that joins both sides of a symmetrical shape.
- Reflection symmetry is where there are one or more lines of symmetry.
- Rotation symmetry is a shape that fits itself if it rotates. An equilateral triangle has a rotational order of three. A square has a rotational order of four. If a given shape only fits once, it has no rotation symmetry.
- Don't be caught out by a wonky rectangle/square. These have no lines of symmetry and are therefore not symmetrical.

Ideas for Design

Art students may explore symmetry by placing a small mirror edge-on over various objects or images and see the resultant shape. The mirror can be moved around over the object to get countless ideas for symmetrical shapes. Students may also wish to explore natural or everyday objects that have symmetrical aspects in order to find ideas for their artwork or designs. Examples may be insects, starfish, crabs, playing cards, scissors, tin openers and stained glass windows.

The students may initially explore the simplest forms of symmetry, as in mirror symmetry, to the more complex, as in objects with more than one line of symmetry, and those with rotational symmetry.

Producing Symmetry in Painting

For the purposes of differentiation, symmetry in art can be explored if the students wish to incorporate an artistic influence into their designs. Max Escher, Bridget Riley, Pablo Picasso and Henri Matisse are four such examples of artists that have symmetrical aspects to their art. Students may also find inspiration for designs by changing the colour palette of the symmetrical shape.

Symmetry in True

Drawing a symmetrical shape freehand helps exercise both sides of the visual channels. The teacher may instruct students to draw a faint cross, which serves as the central axis of the shape, and to draw the lines outwards from central axes of the cross. Viewing the drawing through a mirror or turning it upside down will reveal deviations which may be adjusted as necessary.

Choosing the Palette

Students are free to use the symmetrical shape as they wish within the painting, which might be incorporated into a composition (a butterfly in a wildlife painting) or be a painting in its own right (a motif design). Choice of the colour palette should demonstrate planning, which might be to achieve realism, create a dazzling effect or instill a certain mood.

Symmetry Exploration

Symmetry has such bounds that it could encompass a whole scheme or work or written as a brief. But including it in a single lesson may help students who are unsure of where to begin with a painting, or simply to exercise both sides of the visual channels.

66. Sythnesising Art

Objective 1: To select two art movements for the project.
Objective 2: To write an assignment describing the reasons for the selection.
Objective 3: To produce a painting by combining these two artistic influences.

Students who wish to venture into exploratory art may fuse two artistic styles within a painting. Sampling influences in this way can often yield new ideas or a fresh approach.

Artistic Influences and Movements

Students are spoilt for choice for art movements to choose from, but the following are the most well-known and far reaching.

- Impressionism
- German Expressionism
- Cubism
- Mannerism
- Pre-Raphaelites
- Fauvism
- Surrealism
- Pop Art
- Op Art
- Art Nouveau
- Naïve Art
- Primitive Art

Students are free to select a key painting or the general style of an artist from each art movement. The teacher may first set an assignment to help students focus upon their project. The assignment should be around 1000 words long and answer the following:

1. Describe the two artistic approaches you have selected for your project.
2. Describe briefly a little background into the art movements, including a description of the style and the key artists.
3. Give reasons to why you have chosen these artistic influences.
4. Give a summary of your planned approach to your painting, which should cover: the subject matter, the technique, the effect intended and the purpose of the painting.
5. Reflect upon the project. What went to plan and what didn't? If you were to repeat the exercise, what would you do differently?

New Ideas from Old

Students will discover after poring over art books and other visual resources, that many artistic approaches can be incorporated into their artwork; Seurat's pointillism or Pollock's paint splashes are two contrasting approaches. Similarly, combing the bright colours of the Fauves with the dramatic lighting of Mannerism could yield unprecedented results.

A Painting with Two Sides

The purpose of the exercise is to encourage students to sample art influences and approaches that might be unfamiliar. Such exploration may yield unexpected results and spur inspiration for several further exploratory paintings. For this reason, two or more art lessons, or indeed an entire scheme of work, may need to be dedicated to this project.

67. Introduction to Abstract Painting

Objective 1: To write a 1000 word evaluation on a chosen abstract painting.
Objective 2: To produce an abstract piece of work by using the aforementioned painting as influence.

Venturing into abstract art can seem daunting for students who habitually produce realism. However, experimenting with colour and shape for its own sake can help loosen up artistic style or liberate one from prescriptive aims.

Exploration into Abstract Art

The teacher may begin the lesson by chairing a short discussion on what students think abstract art is. Various phrases and terminology are likely to be: random marks, bright colours, moods, expression, patterns, shapes and so forth. Students may compare these suggestions with authorative art books which might offer further suggestions. The information may be collated and used within a written assignment on a chosen abstract painting.

The teacher may set the research assignment which may be completed at home if time is a factor. Art books, dictionaries and authorative websites can be used to satisfy the following questions:

- In your own words, give a definition of abstract art.
- Select an abstract painting to emulate or draw inspiration. Give the title, artist, art movement and a little background into the painting.
- Give reasons for your selection of this painting.
- Give a description of the painting: the colours used, the lines, the shapes within and painting technique.
- If the painting instills mood, describe.
- Why do you think the artist chose the colours, composition or technique in the painting?
- On completion of your abstract painting, evaluate the experience. Does your painting convey the mood intended? Did the technique go to plan? What went wrong and why? What would you do differently next time?

Abstract Influence

Students may use the results of their research to decide on how to complete their painting. Abstract art from such movements as Expressionism and Cubism can be used. Artists that might provide inspiration are suggested to be:

Picasso, Kandinski, Miro, Kokoschka, Riley, Vasarely, Rothko, Mondrian, Warhol and Pollock.

Artistic Influences

Students who are unsure of where to begin may have a go at taking a line for a walk (chapters 17 and 18), which involves making random marks onto the painting surface and then filling in enclosed spaces with complementary colours. Other students may embark upon an abstract painting by using the chosen influence and think about:

- The mood conveyed. Warm colours instill a different mood to cool colours, as does high colour contrast and harmonious hues.

- The focal point of the painting which might be created by placing an element of a different hue, tone or visual texture to the surrounding area.
- The visual channels of the painting, or the intended pathways throughout the composition.
- The art technique selected, to create a desired effect, whether this is to suggest organic textures or an industrially smooth finish.

Ideas for Further Exploration

Students may use stencils, oil painting mediums and other resources to obtain a particular result.

Like symmetry, abstract art could encompass a whole scheme or work or written as a brief, but would serve well as a taster lesson on abstract art for students who have never encountered this way of expression in their art. Differentiation can easily be provided in the form of the complexity of the composition, the technique chosen and the artistic influence.

68. The Golden Section

Objective 1: To explain what the golden section is.
Objective 2: To devise a painting composition that adheres to the golden section rule.

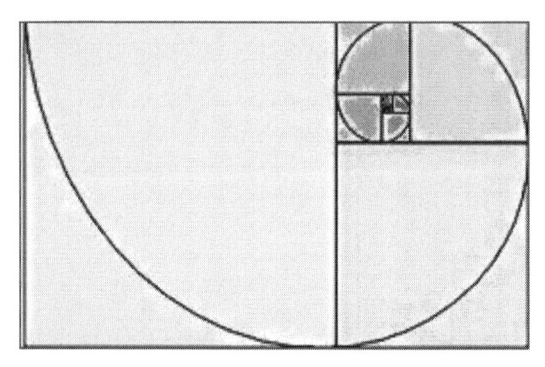

The golden section is a special ratio that when applied to a painting composition, creates a well-balanced painting with perfectly-spaced focal points. Lauded paintings and structures of nature, for that matter, happens to fit this ratio, but what is the golden section?

A Balanced Composition

Students may agree (or not, as the case may be) that placing a focal point dead centre of a painting creates a jarring effect. When asked for a more preferable position, just off-centre feels visually more comfortable. In fact, when examining imagery of such artists as Da Vinci, Picasso and other great artists, such placing of focal points is found to adhere to this rule.

Definition of the Golden Section

the teacher may explain that the golden section can be determined by drawing a square, and then adding an extension to this square to a ratio of 1:1.618 (or phi), as shown on the diagram.

The golden section itself can be similarly subdivided to create its own golden section, and so on. A feature or object that intersects or falls upon any of the resultant lines becomes significant in the painting.

Composing Objects

Students may examine various paintings that look "right" to the eye to establish whether the focal points within fit into this ratio.

It must be noted that a focal point need not necessarily comprise an object, but part of an object, a shadow, a chromatic division or a splash of light.

Students will need rulers and pencils for the following exercise:

On the painting surface, faintly draw a square to fill one side.
Add an extension to this square to a ratio of 1:1.618. If the square is 10cm in size, then an extension of 6.18cm should be added to one side. Calculators will be needed if the measurement is not so easily determined. The resultant extension can be extended again, as shown on the diagram. Students will be left with a painting surface exhibiting several lines.

Composition Deviser

Students may devise a composition by placing significant elements where these lines adjoin, which might be a tree, the highlight on an eggcup or the edge of a curtain. Placing what may seem to be insignificant elements onto these sections could create unexpected focal points. What might seem an uninteresting aspect may suddenly draw the eye. The resultant composition may be used for a future painting.

XIII End of Course Preparation and Assessment

69. Setting Written Assignments

Objective: To write an assignment as directed by the teacher.

Writing assignments to compliment the painting experience serves several purposes, but most crucially gives evidence that learning has taken place. This means the teacher is able to assess the student properly and use the assignment as part of the assessment process.

Literacy in Art

In the past few years, the key skills initiative has raised the profile of literacy. This includes leisure subjects such as art, where written activities become a requisite. But from the students' point of view, putting ideas into words has been shown to enhance learning, helps reflection and aids problem solving. Completing written projects also practices research skills, study skills, organisation and simply using the written word.

A Suitable Assignment

The teacher must take careful consideration to ensure the following when conceiving the assignment brief:

That the assignment reflects the level of the course. For example, an assignment requesting an in-depth evaluation of how the golden section was used within the Renaissance period would not be fitting for a group of beginners. Chapter 10 on Bloom's Taxonomy illustrates the different levels of thought and can be used as a guide.

The assignment must fit the institution's curriculum (if applicable). The assignment must also be relevant to or supports the scheme of work in that it enhances the lesson plans.

The assignment overview must be sufficiently clear that all students understand what is expected of them. Again, chapter 10 may be referred to here, but the mnemonic SMART is relevant and stands for: specific, measurable, attainable, realistic and time-bound. This means that each criterion of the assignment must be clear and realistic given the time frame, the resources available and the students' level of learning.

Opportunities for students to enhance their assignment marking must be given, such as if the student combines two ideas or self-evaluates the assignment or evidences great depth with the research.

The following will also be needed:

- A deadline date.
- The number of words required.
- The format (whether handwritten or printed version is preferred.)
- Other information such as the name of the student, the title of the assignment and question numbers.
- A bibliography.

Assignment Exemplar

The following example of an assignment brief is designed for a class of beginners who are exploring the theme "manmade objects in art" for a scheme of working on still life painting.

Title of Assignment: Manmade Objects in Art

Manmade objects such as jugs, candlesticks and books have been expressed within still life by artists such as Chagall, Cezanne and Gruber. Select a manmade object featured in art and answer the following:

- The name of the object.
- The title of three paintings where it appears including the name of the artist(s) and the time period.
- Give a brief background into each painting. Whether it forms a part of a series or if it was commissioned for a particular occasion.
- In each case, describe the colours used for the object, identify the art technique used and the object's immediate surroundings. Provide information on any symbolic meaning the object might have for the times.
- Describe the differences between how the object has been portrayed in each painting.
- If you were to asked to paint the object, which approach would you use and why.

Number of words: 1000.
Deadline: 12 April 2012.
Supply a bibliography.
No typos please.
Late submissions will achieve no higher than a pass.

Tutorial for Assignments

Logical thought and strategic planning must be evidenced within the assignment but the teacher may give pointers on how students may enhance the overall marking – by evidencing higher cognitive thought, for example. This might be in the form of a reflection upon what the student has learned from the assignment or how a future assignment might be conducted. Good presentation is also vital.

70. Presenting Artwork

Objective: To present artwork for assessment.

The quality of artwork is crucial for the final assessment marking. However, this could go to waste if the art student does not take proper thought and consideration over its presentation. This means banishing grubby finger marks, garish mount card, unevenly-hung paintings and tatty frames.

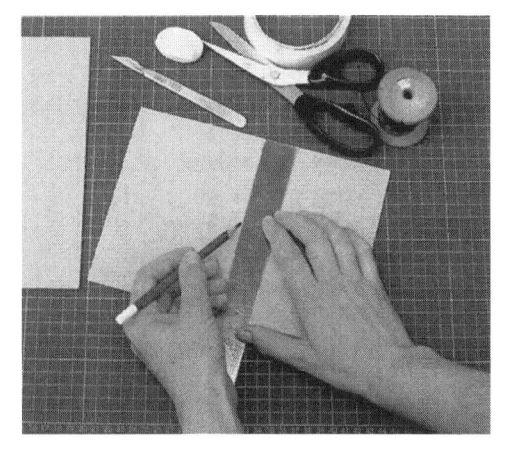

The teacher may offer the following guidelines.

Check List for the Exhibition Space

If the works are to be hung in an exhibition space, the area should be cleaned of any grubby marks and if possible receive a fresh coat of paint.

Sketch out the exhibitions space and work out which paintings will go where. Be sure to hang the best works in the most prominent place. Ensure the works are evenly hung avoiding areas of overcrowding or sparseness. Standing back will help gain an overall feel for the exhibition.

Restrictions may apply, but consider using spotlights around the art space to add ambience. Mobile versions with suction caps can be strategically placed around the area to enhance the viewing experience.

Framing

Take special consideration over framing. Wide wooden frames will add a rustic feel to traditional oil paintings; contemporary artwork will benefit from a minimal surround. Shopping around for frames from craft fairs or car boots may reward the student with old, unusual or antique frames with which to dress up the artwork. The paintings may be varnished prior to framing. A guide on varnishing oils can be found in chapter 72.

The Portfolio

Inserting good quality photographs of artwork into a large plastic wallet will serve well as an artist's portfolio and keeps work clean. Never use scissors to trim photos, but a scalpel and metal ruler. Spray mount or double sided tape will ensure the images stay in place. Guidance on taking good photographs of paintings can be found next.

Presenting Artwork

Take special consideration over plaques, labels and printed text. Avoid using fancy or small fonts and keep text to a minimum to avoid detracting from the artwork. Mounting text onto card will yield a professional finish. Using strong double-sided tape on the back will dispense with the need for messy-looking cellotape or blue tack.

Coursework

Developmental work and sketches can be collated within a large folder to show evidence of how the visual conclusion(s) were reached. The written assignment should be placed in a plastic wallet to keep the work clean.

Most importantly, label all works, portfolios and the written assignments with the student's name and the title of the project.

71. Photographing Paintings

Objective: To produce photographs of artwork as directed by the teacher.

A portfolio of poorly-photographed paintings could put to waste high detail and vivid colours of the actual painting. But the teacher may advise students on how to take optimum quality photographs for the purposes of assessment, interview or a portfolio.

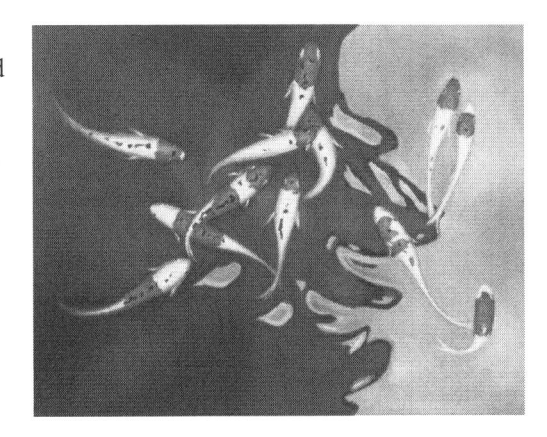

Tricks for Optimum Photography

Avoid using a flash for it will bounce from the varnish and bleach out the colours of the painting. Similarly, beware of reflections caused by nearby windows or white surfaces.

The best lighting is natural daylight on a bright cloudy day, when the light is most diffuse. A daylight bulb may alternatively be used, but avoid household bulbs that cast a yellowish hue. A tripod may be necessary.

Take several photographs of the painting using various shutter speeds and light settings to offer a choice of photographs.

Look out for bright lights behind the painting that could fog out the edges. Draping a dark cloth behind the painting will prevent this from happening.

The painting will look distorted if the photo is taken too close to it. Similarly never use a wide lens setting. It is best to stand well back and use an ordinary lens setting or a telephoto lens. Beware that some digital cameras have a zoom function that merely crops the view to make it look close-up. The resultant photograph will have poor definition.

Allow some of the background to show around the painting so that the image can be cropped when using photographic software.

Ensure the setting is on optimum resolution setting. Portrait mode on most digital cameras is usually best.

Squeeze the shutter release gently to avoid camera shake during the shot. In poor light, use a tripod.

Presentation of Photos

Mounting photographs onto card will protect them from damage and give a professional finish. Avoid garish colours. Creams, beiges, light greens or blues are the safest bet for retaining the photos' focal point, whilst enhancing their presentation.

72. Varnishing the Oil Paintings

Objective 1: To recite the main types of varnishes.
Objective 2: To varnish oil paintings where necessary.

Varnishing an oil painting provides the finishing touches, as it restores the painting's original "wet" look, making colours appear renewed and thus enhancing the viewing experience.

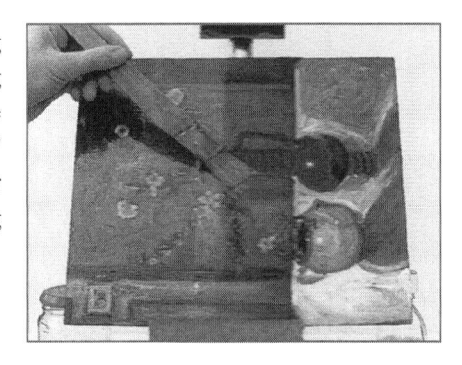

Why Varnish?

Students do not have to varnish their paintings, as oils take months to dry anyway, but for informative purposes, the teacher may offer advice for students wishing to varnish their works.

Varnish offers a defense against dust, damp and debris. Providing a tough layer, it also helps protect the painting surface against abrasions and knocks, which can easily occur during transit and the hanging of oil paintings.

Types of Varnishes

There are several types of varnishes on the market. For an antique finish, organic varnishes such as dammar varnish and mastic varnish can be used, but these can be expensive. Modern synthetic varnishes can be purchased at more reasonable prices.

Retouching varnish will provide a protective layer for paintings that are not quite dry. Retouching varnish can easily be removed with an artist's solvent or special varnish remover, if required. Spraying varnish is ideal for particularly vulnerable paintings.

Shiny Versus Matt

Varnishes can be narrowed down to matt varnish, most often used for contemporary and abstract art; gloss for traditional fine art or satin for an effect somewhere in between. Spraying varnish can be used for an extra smooth finish.

Where to Varnish

The area designated for varnishing must be free of dust, dirt and drafts. The varnishing brush must also be clean and soft. For this reason, it would be a good idea to place the artwork in a quiet room where the varnish will be allowed to dry without disturbances in the atmosphere. Avoid direct sunlight and allow ventilation.

Varnish Application

Ensure the painting is thoroughly dry prior to varnishing. Traditional oil paintings require at least three months or more but a light coat of retouching varnish will solve the problem. Alkyd paints or oils completed with an alkyd medium dry rapidly and require a few weeks.

A little varnish should firstly be poured into a separate jar with a wide lip. This ensures the rest of the varnish remains pure, should a little dust or dirt get on the brush. Lightly dip the bristle ends into the varnish – overloading the brush should be avoided. To attain an even layer, brush briskly in all directions, keeping the brush moving.

Parts missed can be revealed by holding the painting up to a light source and looking for areas that lack lustre. These areas can be worked over. The painting should be allowed to dry for at least twenty four hours lying flat. A second coat may sometimes be necessary if the surface retains dull patches. Varnishing brushes should be cleaned in solvents or warm soapy water immediately afterwards.

73. Preparing the Summative Assessment

Objective 1: To agree goals with students.
Objective 2: To inform students of their progress.

Not all leisure courses have a summative assessment, but most do, and it serves to give students something to aim for at the end of the course module and to inform on how they have developed artistically. However few students like obtaining a certain mark and not know why, for this may cause unwanted surprises or a shock. This is why it is a good idea to conduct a mock assessment informing students of their progress track, what they expect to achieve and giving them the chance to put right issues.

A mock assessment may occur at any time within the last half of the course; it is really up to the teacher to decide. It is a good idea to ensure the rest of the class are busy on a current project whilst the teacher discusses each student's work in a private place, which might be in the corner of the room. Time-keeping is essential – twenty minutes or so often suffices, but may overflow into the next lesson.

Agreeing Goals

Praise firstly. Praise anything the student has done well, has shown effort with or has achieved despite difficulty. Afterwards, point out any issues that may cause concern, such as the following:

- Projects running behind schedule.
- Missing projects.
- Work that does not evidence some or any of the criteria set out, such as research work or experimentation.
- Frequent absences.

The student may agree to complete a project or painting by an allotted time or write a creative log to enhance the assessment marking. Under special circumstances, the teacher may allow a deadline extension to complete a project.

With everything discussed, I will write up the agreed goals in front of the student, including areas for concern, projected marking as things stand, and what the final marking could be if certain actions were taken. Putting things into black and white serves to clarify what has been discussed and make them more concrete. Unexpected surprises and nasty shocks are kept in check.

74. The Summative Assessment

Assessing artwork without a subjective view can be difficult, which is why the assessment criteria should be made clear on the first session of the course, and a copy supplied to each student in the form of a brief (chapter 9). Some or any of the following may be used within a course requirement.

- Evidence of creative use of materials.
- Competent use of mediums.
- Research work.
- Experimental and/or developmental work.
- Participation in tutorials and critiques.
- Written work such as project proposals, essays and dissertations.
- A creative log.
- A presentation.
- Completed artwork.
- At least 80% attendance.

But the following outline the typical requirements to pass a single painting module:

- A creative diary evidencing self-evaluation. This might be in the form of a reflective log of the student's aims, problems encountered and how solutions were found during the creative process.
- 2 pieces of experimental and/or developmental work.
- 1000 word assignment as outlined on the project brief.
- The final artwork.

As can be seen from this example, the criteria should be SMART, like the objectives discussed in chapter 10, in that each must reflect the level of the course, the time frame given, the resources available, be specific and measureable. The assessment should also be focused only on the subject at hand. For example, marks should not be deducted from a research assignment that fulfils all the criteria if the handwriting is untidy; the criterion is not hand dexterity, but the content of the assignment.

The teacher may warn students however that an attendance of less than the stated amount or late submission of work will at best attain a pass, regardless of the quality of the artwork or the assignment. Missing work will award a fail.

Conducting the Assessment

Students may be given an allotted time to attend the assessment with all the work as set out in the criteria requirement. The agreement as set out in the mock assessment may be referred to if necessary or appropriate. Again, praise whenever the opportunity arises. The final marking should never be a surprise and the student should be informed on exactly why a particular marking has been awarded. The teacher may write a short feedback on the student's work, relating to the creative use of materials, the painting style and willingness to try new ideas.

Student Evaluation

The student has the opportunity to write a feedback on the learning experience, which might include the teaching, the resources or the institution's policies. The teacher may collate this information and use it for self-evaluation, to be discussed in the following chapter. Recurrent themes may crop up, which might highlight a need for change. The feedback may inform on anything relating to the learner's experience within the module and indeed can be invaluable to the teacher.

75. The Purpose of Evaluation

No art lesson, scheme of work or assessment goes to plan, and if things go wrong, which as often they do, the teacher may reflect upon what actions can be taken to improve things. Feedback from any source, particularly the students, can be invaluable. The following issues, or trigger incidences, may cause a teacher to critically think.

The resources create difficulty, for example, the studio easels are tatty and malfunction, the room is small, the chairs are not comfortable or the artificial lighting causes unwanted glares.

The activities in the lesson were too advanced for the art group. Or conversely the activities were not challenging enough.

The lesson plan did not take into account the speed at which the students work, meaning some finish before others and have nothing to do. Perhaps there are not enough activities within the lesson plan to keep students occupied, or some activities take too long.

Again, a lesson plan that works perfectly for one group may not necessarily work for another. Making provisions for differentiation; the size of the art group and the environment enables the teacher to create a flexible lesson plan to suit.

But making such changes for improvement is achievable only by employing the reflective cycle.

The Kolb Cycle

David Kolb (1984) believed that learning could only occur when the reflective cycle has taken place or in other words, improvement can only occur from past failures. The reflective cycle consists of four stages. These are: concrete experience, reflection, abstract conceptualisation and active experimentation. The experience is the task at hand without any reflection or cognitive thought. Once the experience has happened, the teacher might reflect upon it. This involves stepping back and reviewing what has gone wrong (or right, for that matter). The third stage is abstract conceptualisation which involves actively making adjustments, modifying and making necessary changes. Only when these three stages are complete can the experimentation stage commence. This involves taking the changes and embedding them into the practice. The cycle is complete.

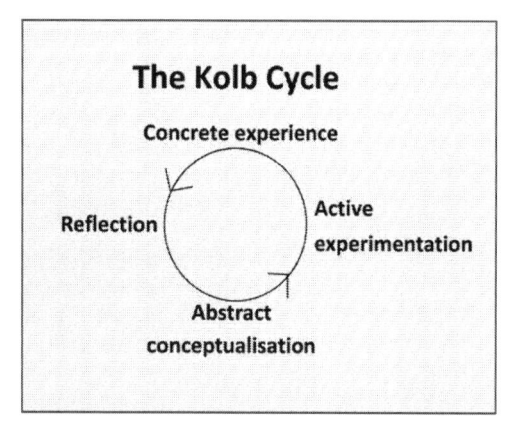

The Kolb Cycle

Concrete experience

Reflection

Active experimentation

Abstract conceptualisation

The reflective or "learning" cycle might be repeated many times, each time, involving small increments of improvement. According to Kolb, everything practiced in mankind must go through the reflective cycle for the practice to improve. Without the reflective cycle, learning and improvement cannot take place. Similarly, the Kolb cycle will help the teacher (and the students) find solutions.

Finding Solutions after Reflection

As a result of reflection, the teacher might move the furniture around, add more art activities, suggest students bring lamps, make an official request for replacement easels or simply get advice. Again, things may not go to plan, which will make more reflection necessary. It is a good idea to keep a log after every lesson, putting into writing how the lesson went and focusing on issues. Going through the four stages of the reflective cycle may help find solutions, and the log may also be referred to when looking for patterns or relating past problems to the present.

XIV After-matter

Health & Safety for Art Classes

Preparing oil painting lessons often involves a session on health and safety. This not only entails the college's rules on fire practice and sensible conduct in corridors, but safe practice of the art materials themselves. In this regard, health and safety exists on two levels: college-wise, and class-wise.

Safety Policies in Institutions

Every educational institute has its own safety procedures in place, so the teacher must obtain these guidelines from administration regarding fire drill, what to do in case of accident, a point of contact should injury occur and how to complete the accident log. The following is a typical example of health and safety procedures if a student is injured in class.

- Do not administer first aid unless qualified to do so.
- In the event of serious injury, do not attempt to move the injured person or offer anything to eat or drink.
- No member of staff is allowed to give any medicine including painkillers. If the problem is serious, the college will call an ambulance.
- Ensure that the college has a contact name and a number in case of emergencies.
- Accidents in class should always be reported to the tutor so that the appropriate forms can be completed and the accident investigated.
- It is the student's responsibility to become familiar with and comply with all instructions codes of practice or notices which the college has in place.
- Ask for assistance from a member of staff, first aid or reception.

Safe Studio Practice

When it comes to safe practice in the art studio, the teacher may have to prepare a separate health and safety sheet. The following may help give the teacher an idea of what is involved and help minimise the probability of having to fill in an accident form in art class.

- Ensure the floor is free is spillages.
- Ensure all art equipment, such as art boxes or easels do not pose a tripping risk.
- Do not attempt to lift heavy equipment if a medical condition exists.
- Store solvents, varnishes and aerosol cans in a cool place away from heat or direct sunlight.
- Avoid using spray varnishes in a confined room.
- Avoid skin contact with substances that may cause a known allergy.
- Ensure that easels are properly erected and steady.
- Switch off overhead projectors at the end of lesson.
- Prefer plastic containers to glass. If glass is brought to class, take extra care.

Risk Assessment

If the classes are to be conducted in another capacity, such as a hall or private residence, a risk assessment will be necessary. Risk assessments ensure the area adheres to health and safety regulations. The following will be taken into account:

- Electrical equipment is maintained.
- Fire equipment is in working order.
- Fire exits are kept clear and that personnel and students know the drill.
- Personnel are aware of additional safety policies.
- A point of contact at all times for first aid.

- That the teacher is aware of any health problems of the students.
- Procedures for filling in the accident book.

Safety in Art Class

Conducting a series of lessons in oil painting, as with any course, will inevitably involve preparing and delivering a health and safety session. Each college will have its own procedures in place regarding fire drill and conduct in corridors. A risk assessment will be necessary in any other capacity. In both cases, the art teacher may have to prepare a separate health and safety sheet regarding the art materials concerned. This will help mininise the event of accidents in class.

Glossary

Aims or outcomes: in teaching context are generalised statements of intent that stand for what a student or teacher hopes to achieve at the end of the session.

Andragogy: A method of teaching that is student-centred, flexible and humanistic. It encourages independent learning and cognitive thought (the opposite to pedagogy).

Acrylic paint: A water-soluble paint made from a polymer.

Acrylic primer: A water-soluble paint that dries water-resistant, designed to seal the painting support prior to the oil painting. Acrylic primer is sometimes known as "acrylic gesso."

Alkyd: A synthetic resin that can be added to oil paint to accelerate its drying time. Alkyds are also a type of paint designed for glazing techniques as they are translucent and dry quickly.

Alla prima: A painting completed in one go as opposed to layers.

Assessment: A means of charting and measuring students' learning. Initial assessments occur prior to the course, formative assessments occur during the course, and a summative assessment occurs at the end. Assessments come in the form of tests, quizzes and practical exercises.

Ausubel's Subsumption Theory: Named after the Cognitivist, David Ausubel, a means of assimilating information in a logical and hierarchical order from the simple to the complex starting with the shortest and easiest tasks, progressing to the more difficult. Regular signposting and consolidation serve as learning reinforcement.

Behaviourism: A mode of behaviour that is learned without cognitive processes. In context of the classroom, the behaviourist model is teacher-directed, concrete and highly-structured. This is also known as pedagogy.

Bloom's Taxonomy: Name after Benjamin Bloom, classifications of cognitive thought that follow thus: recall, comprehend, apply, analyse, synthesise and evaluate. Each describes progressively more advanced ways of thinking.

Bristle: A stiff brush such as hog hair for robust brushwork and impasto.

Cognitivism: In terms of the classroom, a mode of learning that results from conscious thought processes, for example by reflection, analysis or critical thinking.

Complementary colour: A colour situated on the opposite segment to any given colour on the colour wheel. Red, for example is the complementary to green.

Differentiation: A means of making the lesson plan inclusive so that all students of all abilities are able to take part in the activities.

Gesso: Chalk whiting suspended in glue which is applied to the painting support prior to oil painting.

Glaze: A thin, translucent layer of paint usually diluted with artist solvent and/or oil mediums.

Golden section: A segment that extends a square to the ratio of 1:1.618. The segment can itself be subdivided to this ratio. An object or feature that falls upon the resultant lines becomes significant within a composition.

Impasto: The application of thick paint.

Impasto medium: An alkyd-based medium that adds bulk to paint for impasto techniques.

Individual learning plan (or ILP): A personalised and flexible learning route for a student who has special needs to achieve a given goal.

Kolb Cycle: Otherwise known as the reflective cycle. These consist of concrete experience (the incident), reflection (what went wrong?), abstract conceptualisation (making changes) and active experimentation (putting the changes into practice). By completing these four stages, problem solving and improvements can be made.

Learning mentor: An aid that assists special needs students with domestic tasks in the classroom.

Learning styles: Modes of receiving information, which might be visual, auditory or kinaesthetic. A multi sensory lesson plan engaging all three channels has been found to help students learn more effectively.

Linseed oil: Extracted from the linseed, the carrier of oil paint. When used as a medium, it adds gloss, transparency and flow.

Liquin: An alkyd-based medium that accelerates the drying process of oil paint. Liquin provides a non-glossy alternative to linseed oil.

Negative shape: the background and foreground area surrounding the main subject matter.

Objectives: in context of teaching, a specific statement describing what students will have achieved by the end of class. Objectives must be SMART-friendly (see SMART).

Pedagogy: A method of teaching that is teacher-centred, highly-directed and structured (the opposite to andragogy).

Pochade box: A small box with slotted compartments and an angled lid for transportation of art materials and wet paintings.

Primary colour: A fundamental colour that cannot be made from the mixture of other colours. In terms of printing ink, the primaries are magenta, cyan and yellow.

Sable: A soft brush made from the fur of the sable, a small mammal.

Scheme of work: Also known as a programme of study. A series of coherent lessons that form a module.

Scumbling: The application of thin but neat paint, to produce a broken glaze.

Sgraffito: The method of etching into the paint surface whilst it is still wet to reveal another glaze beneath.

SMART objectives: A mnemonic that stands for specific, measurable, attainable, realistic and time-bound. A useful checklist for teachers writing objectives to ensure that each is well-suited to the learners and the class.

Solvent: A thinner for oil paint. Solvents are also used for cleaning the brushes.

Varnish: A transparent, hard drying solution that is applied onto an oil painting once it is dry. This protects the painting from damp and dirt.

Wet-into-wet: The application of wet paint to a wet glaze.

Suggested Further Reading & Resources

Some of the following supply suitable visual resources for art, others are handy little books for teachers to carry around. The rest offer more in-depth guidance on teaching methods and art.

Armitage, Andy, et al: (2003) *Teaching and Training in Post Compulsory Education*, Open University Press

Collings, Matthew: (1999) *This is Modern Art*, Weidenfeld & Nicolson

Cumming, Robert: (2005) *Eyewitness Companions Art*, Dorling Kindersley

Curzon, L. B.: (2004) *Teaching in Further Education*, Fulton

Edwards, Betty: (2001) *Drawing on the Right Side of the Brain*, HarperCollins

Gardner, Howard: (2011) *Frames of Mind: The Theory of Multiple Intelligences*, Basic Books

Lynton, Norbert: (1980) *The Story of Modern Art*, Book Club Associates

Macpherson, Kevin: 2000 *Fill your Oil Painting with Light and Colour*: place, North Light Books

Petty, Geoff: (2004) *Teaching Today, a Practical Guide*, Nelson Thornes

Reece, Ian and Walker, Stephen: 2003 *Teaching, Training and Learning, a Practical Guide*, Business Education Publishers Ltd

Smith, Stan and Wheeler, Linda: (1983) *Drawing and Painting the Figure*, Tiger Books International

Welton, Jude: (1993) *Eyewitness Art Impressionism* Dorling Kindersley

Welton, Jude: (1994) *Eyewitness Art Looking at Paintings* Dorling Kindersley

About the Author

I attained a Bachelor of Arts Degree at Kingston University, Surrey, and attained my PCET teaching qualification from Warwick University, Warwickshire.

I have taught life drawing, painting, drawing and textiles at my local college. My specialist subject remains with oil painting, and I have completed countless projects, commissions and written numerous articles on the subject of art and teaching art. See my bibliography below:

Art books

Why do My Clouds Look like Cotton Wool? (2011) Oil Painting Medic
Why do My Ellipses Look like Doughnuts? (2011) Oil Painting Medic
Why do My Skin Tones Look Lifeless? (2012) Oil Painting Medic
Landscape Painting in Oils, 20 Step by Step Guides (2011) Oil Painting Medic
The Artist's Garden in Oils, 18 Step by Step Guides (2012) Oil Painting Medic
Portrait Painting in Oil, 10 Step by Step Guides (2012) Oil Painting Medic
How Can I Inspire my Painting Class? Lesson Plan Ideas for Oil Painting in Post Compulsory Education and an Essential Guide to Teaching (colour and black and white edition) (2011) Oil Painting Medic
Draw What You See Not What You Think You See (212) Oil Painting Medic
Oil Paintings from your Garden (2002) Guild of Master Craftsman Limited.
Oil Paintings from the Landscape (2003) Guild of Master Craftsman Limited.

Children's picture books:

Ben's Little Big Adventure (2011) Rachel Shirley
Katie's Magic Teapot and the Cosmic Pandas (2011) Rachel Shirley
Katie and the Cosmic Pandas' Deep Sea Voyage (2011) Rachel Shirley

Printed in Germany
by Amazon Distribution
GmbH, Leipzig